Massimo Recalcati

The Enduring Kiss

Seven Short Lessons on Love

Translated by Alice Kilgarriff

polity

Copyright © Giangiacomo Feltrinelli Editore, Milano
First published in 2019 with the title *Mantieni il bacio*
Published under licence from Giangiacomo Feltrinelli Editore, Milan, Italy

This English edition © Polity Press, 2021

Polity Press
65 Bridge Street
Cambridge CB2 1UR, UK

Polity Press
101 Station Landing
Suite 300
Medford, MA 02155, USA

ISBN-13: 978-1-5095-4248-2
ISBN-13: 978-1-5095-4249-9 (paperback)

A catalogue record for this book is available from the British Library.

Typeset in 12 on 15 pt Fournier MT by
Servis Filmsetting Ltd, Stockport, Cheshire
Printed and bound in Great Britain by TJ Books Limited

The publisher has used its best endeavours to ensure that the URLs for external websites
referred to in this book are correct and active at the time of going to press. However, the
publisher has no responsibility for the websites and can make no guarantee that a site will
remain live or that the content is or will remain appropriate.

Every effort has been made to trace all copyright holders, but if any have been overlooked the
publisher will be pleased to include any necessary credits in any subsequent reprint or edition.

For further information on Polity, visit our website:
politybooks.com

To Roberto Benigni, who understands the
poetry of endurance

Contents

Acknowledgements

My warmest thanks to Stefano Coletta, the director of Rai 3, for having believed in the power of the word and having challenged the stifling stereotypes of commercial television with a decidedly anti-televisual programme, reiterating the social and civil role of public television. Thanks also to Gianluca Foglia, who since *The Telemachus Complex* has been a valued interlocutor of mine. And last but not least, to Arianna Bayre, who unwittingly provided me with the right words.

Introduction

The title of this book comes from a dream I once had. The day before, my Pilates teacher Arianna, who has long helped me to mend my poor back worn out by thirty years of practising psychoanalysis, had given me a particular exercise to do. Lying on my back and holding my knees together, I had to rotate one leg at a time. Whilst holding this uncomfortable and unnatural posture, Arianna told me to 'maintain the kiss' between my knees, which the leg rotation tended to break. 'Massimo', she told me sternly, 'maintain the kiss.'

In the dream, this day residue (as Freud would define it) developed in a surprising way. At that time, I had a provisional title for this book that I was not entirely happy with, and my dream developed both the day residue of the Pilates lesson and this dissatisfaction. In the dream I am at the Fondazione Feltrinelli in Milan. I am striding up the stairs to the floor where the publishing house is. No one is there apart from the editorial director, who is waiting for me in his office. I am meeting him to tell him the title of my next book, which will be '*Enduring Kiss*'. His reaction is incredibly positive. Then he asks me, 'Where does it come from?' I answer, 'The same place as the others.' 'Which is?', he asks. 'My unconscious.'

I wake up with a feeling of childlike happiness and a new title for my book, one that I am entirely happy with.

The kiss is the image that, perhaps more than any other, encompasses the beauty and poetry of love. It's no coincidence that the kiss doesn't feature in contractual love; even in pornography it is rare. The kiss is a moment of intimacy that unites the place of the word and that of the body in a remarkable way. If there is no love without a declaration of love, equally there is no love without a kiss. If there is no love without you or I saying 'I love you', there can never be love without a kiss.

Every love is required to maintain the kiss, to make it last. Only the kiss joins the tongue that declares love with the body of the lover. There is no loving kiss that doesn't involve the tongue. We are well aware of this. It is the tongue that distinguishes a loving kiss from other kinds of kisses. One can kiss a child, a friend, a sibling or parent with affection, but only the presence of the tongue implies the eroticism of desire.

Love binds this eroticism – the eroticism of the tongue, of the kiss 'of' or 'with' the tongue, that can also be simply sexual or sensual – to the declaration of love, to the words of love, to their declaration: 'I love you.' Every loving kiss, always and silently, declares 'I love you.' It is from the silence of the tongue that the kiss's declaration of love emerges. To feel the beloved's tongue is like feeling their heartbeat: it is the declaration of my love, it makes love exist. It is like making love.

Whilst I maintain the kiss, I touch your tongue, your voice, your word, your name. Whilst I maintain the kiss, I transform your body into a new language and a new alphabet. I feel the whole history of your body deposited on the unique mystery that is your tongue. I feel all the life I have lived pass into this new tongue that we have now become.

So, I maintain the kiss; I trap it in memory and time. Your tongue like roses or caramel, like rain or snow, like sea or wind. Your tongue like a new frontier. I tie and untie myself from the memory of all the times and first kisses I have experienced. I discover my body is made to be opened up, to host a new tongue and to combine mine with yours. I discover that my body is exposed to the new event of your unpronounceable tongue.

This is the immense joy of the Two, when it occurs: feeling your entire body in your tongue. Learning to talk in a new way. Learning a new presence in me. Experiencing the tongue that, like the world, is born once more.

The kiss does not unite. It doesn't penetrate, it doesn't meld the lovers into a single body. In the kiss, the bodies stay divided, separate, distinct. The intimacy of the kiss causes One to fall deeply into the Other, but the bodies remain Two.

Rather, it is only because the bodies remain Two that the kiss is possible. A rapid descent of the stairs or a mountain valley, of a drop onto the sea. The plunging heart.

I kiss you as if wrapped in a spring breeze, and I pour my whole tongue, my entire world, my very being into you. My whole being is in the tongue that kisses you and talks to you. I am in every point of your mouth, of your voice, of your body, of the unknown words of your tongue.

I maintain the kiss in the dark of night and the light of day. I maintain it in the time that passes. I maintain it in the burning rage of the world, in all its ferociousness. Lovers carve out their hiding holes, finding their peace from war, from the infinite pain of being. When they kiss the noise of the world is silenced, its laws broken, time is stolen from its normal continuity. They fall together in their distinct, embraced tongues.

I carry my first kiss from when I was a boy with me like an amulet. When I kissed the girl for the first time, she tasted of mint. She had pulled close to me in the dark oratory cinema room. Our hearts between us, beating. I had passed a threshold, and no other has ever been so sweet and mysterious. My tongue was in hers. I can still see her half-closed eyes and her face abandoning themselves on my shoulders. I found a tongue I knew nothing about. Did it even have an alphabet? A dictionary? A code?

Though there are long, drawn-out kisses, kissing competitions, Guinness world record kisses, the kiss is only ever fleeting when compared to the love story of the Two. The extinction of the kiss and, most importantly, of the desire to kiss one's beloved is always an indication of a crisis, announcing the imminent demise of love.

To maintain the kiss means keeping the promise of the tongue, the promise of a secret that cannot be dissolved. The foreign and inappropriable nature of the tongue as that of the Other.

In the exercise Arianna asked me to do, a tension that came from the contraction of the abdominal muscles should have kept the knees from drawing apart. Indeed, as she explained, a certain tension is required to ensure an 'enduring kiss', to maintain that kiss. This tension is the same one that overwhelms lovers: will they know how to keep the secret of their foreign tongues? Will they know how to value the direction of their travel, the continual creation and dissolution of their kisses?

You know that when I kiss you, you who did not share that first kiss, you who became my woman, my wife, every one of our kisses is like the first. You know that when I kiss you, I still feel my heart in my tongue like in that first kiss. So, I maintain our kiss, holding my knees tight. I still hold your heart on my tongue and my heart on yours.

Is it really possible to give lessons on love? Obviously not. It is never possible to explain love, never possible to reduce love to a concept. It is, however, possible and necessary to speak of love, to keep on speaking of love, to the point that we can even say speaking of love is the only thing we can do when it comes to love. We speak so much of love because no one knows what it is. This book talks about love using a number of lessons that are not, in fact, lessons at all. It actually comes from a sort of 'script' written for the television series shown on Italy's national broadcaster, Rai 3, entitled *Lessico Amoroso* [*Lexicon of Love*] (January–March 2019). A script that was so extensive, so rich in references, thoughts and themes, that it could not be fully developed using this format, given the fatal limitations of television.

So, here we have a series of seven brief 'lessons' that investigate the mystery and miracle of love, from the contingent event of the encounter to that of its end or its endurance, as mysterious and miraculous as the event of every first encounter.

Milan, January 2019

I

The Promise

Love demands love. [. . .] It demands it . . . *encore*.

Jacques Lacan, *The Seminar of Jacques Lacan: Book XX*

To Burn or To Last?

Does it burn or does it last? If it burns out it consumes itself quickly and cannot last. In order to last it must not burn brightly, but instead lower the intensity of its flame. But what becomes of a love that no longer burns? Can a love still exist when there is no longer fire? Is that love worthy of still being called 'love'? As Roland Barthes asks, why is it better to last than to burn?[1]

The figure of the person in love seems to be different to that of the husband, the figure of the sensual lover different to that of wife and mother. Does the lexicon of the family signal the end of the lexicon of love? On the one hand, we have the fire of the person in love, whilst on the other we have the affectionate presence of the father or husband. On one hand, we have the eroticism of the lover, on the other the attentive care of the wife or mother. One side burns, the other endures. Isn't this perhaps one of love's greatest paradoxes? We will see it in all of its different guises in this book.

We can attempt to grasp things from the outset and simply ask ourselves: how is love born? How does it happen? How is it that the Two meet and declare their love for one another? What is love's secret? What does it mean to declare one's own love? What do we mean when we say, 'I love you'?[2] Is it all a trick, an illusion, a trap, as so many insist? Is it, as the most cynical would have it, a waste of time, a needless pain or an irritation to be ignored? And then, how long does a love last? How long can it last? Doesn't a declaration of love that wants to be forever exist as an irreconcilable contradiction? Doesn't every love necessarily end up in the shit? Doesn't it always eventually end in hate? Isn't this the ultimate truth about love? Doesn't every love always come to an end? Is believing in love between Two akin then to believing in a fairytale? Is declaring one's own love to be 'forever' not a signal of the psychological immaturity of the person making that declaration?

Novalis warned us that the mystery of love cannot be explained; that the only people with any authority to speak about it are poets. Psychoanalysts, on the other hand, are often among the most determined adversaries of love as a promise that demands to last forever. Some of them would say that whoever declares love forever is talking rubbish.[3] And yet in every age and in every corner of the world, the birth of a love defies time because every love worthy of this name would like to be 'forever', would want its flame to be eternal. Every time I say 'I love you' I mean (lovers mean) that 'it will be forever', regardless of any rational evidence or common experience to the contrary. The promise of love is, indeed, a promise that is not afraid of evoking eternity – 'our love will be forever'.

Saying 'I Love You'

Freud did not believe in any way, shape or form in the miracle of love. He insisted that it was the illusory result of a narcissistic passion for one's own I, or rather, one's own narcissistic ideal. He believed that to love means nothing more than to adore one's own ideal image embodied by the beloved. When I say 'I love you', I am saying that 'I love myself through you', I am saying that 'I love myself in you', that 'I love myself', that 'I love my I in you.' The subject is more important than the verb.

Love for Freud is essentially an imaginary phenomenon that belongs to the sphere of narcissism and is consumed among the deceptive reflections of the mirror. He believes that we never love the beloved for what they are but for what we imagine them to be, or more precisely, for the ideal of ourselves that they reflect. What I love in you is my own ideal I, the way in which your gaze looks at me and makes me lovable. Love, for Freud, is always accompanied by narcissistic fantasies. It is a deceptive passion, the effect of the subject in love being blinded and hence overestimating the object of their passion in order to exalt themselves. It is, in short, a mirage. And it exists, contrary to what we might believe, more in the dimension of having, of receiving rather than that of giving, it is more about appropriation than expropriation, about centralization of the self rather than its decentralization. This is why every act of falling in love, fed by the narcissistic fantasy, tends to vanish at the first disappointment, the first experience of non-coincidence between how the beloved is in reality and their ideal-narcissistic representation.

Is love, Freud's critical voice would continue to insist, actually an experience of the New? Of a new life? Of a new experience of the world? Or just illusions, traps, smoke and mirrors created by poets? What if love of the Two was actually nothing more than the repetition of ancient, repressed loves, hidden deep down in our memories? What if it were nothing more than the impression of a mark that has already been left? Nothing but a game of masks? Isn't it true that behind the beloved woman there is always the unconscious shadow of one's own mother? And does the mother (or even – in some rarer cases – the everlasting childhood ideal of the father) not always, even for a woman, overshadow the beloved man? The experience of the unconscious would teach us that love is never love for the New, but only ever the replica of the same love – love for the mother – that condemns us to repeat, in identical forms, the disappointment of the Same. In this way, the spectres of our past, our fantasies, our first experiences of infant sexuality, of our most archaic fears, all fall onto our beloved. Freud would have demonstrated without exception how the so-called New of love is nothing more than a reissuing of the old, of that which has already been, of a love that has already been consumed – with the mother or with the father – and that stops the loving encounter from ever truly being a new one. Rather, love would be a form of psychic regression, returning us to a childlike state in which we either idealize the Other or chastise them for not being as ideal as we had fooled ourselves they were. The skirmishes of love repeat the skirmishes of our most remote childhood fantasies.

The Miracle of the Encounter

But perhaps Freud lacked the words (or the experience – was Freud ever in love?) to describe the generative force that the event of the loving encounter carries with it. Because if we look closely at its beginning, we see love is caused first and foremost by the enchantment of the encounter. Love offers itself not as regression or repetition, but as a surprise. Something unpredicted, unplanned, unexpected occurs that interrupts the sequence of the already-known, the already-been, already-seen. Every loving encounter suspends the natural passing of time; it digs a hole, an empty space, opening up a gap, a discontinuity that we could not have predicted in the usual course of things in the world. In this sense, the encounter always tastes of the future, of that which has never been before, of a festival if the festival is the place where the ordinary is derailed by the explosion of forbidden joy. 'The amorous subject', writes Roland Barthes, 'experiences every meeting with the loved being as a festival.'[4]

The loving encounter always seems like a miracle because it transforms the predictable into the unpredictable, the possible into the impossible, water into wine, routine into revelation. But regardless of whether the promise is miraculous, every loving encounter always occurs by chance. In a supermarket, at a party or through an aquarium, as happens in Baz Luhrmann's *Romeo + Juliet* (1996), in which the gazes of the Two (Leonardo Di Caprio and Claire Danes) meet obliquely, as if by magic, through the clear waters of the aquarium with its multi-coloured fish, and cannot help but follow one another, each drawn to the other like a magnet. The focus here is on just one detail of the body: the gaze. For Lacan, this is the object that corresponds most to the movement of desire. But the encounter is always made up of details, fragments, pieces of the body: looks, scents, the sound of a voice, the colour of hair or eyes, clothes, a silhouette. We never fall in love with souls, but always and only with bodies. I must add here that love usually emerges from a unique flaw of the body rather than from its ideal perfection. Often, a body's perfection has the effect of anaesthetizing love, of rendering the beloved too distant, unreachable, whilst the flaw throws open the lack from which love can emerge, mobilizing the desire that finds this imperfection to be a divine detail. God, as Flaubert and Warburg have rightly said, is in the details. The enchantment of the encounter always implies a mystery. Why with her, why with him? What does this unknown hold, this x that has ignited my desire? The encounter seems to happen as if it were already written, but it never is; it has never, despite what lovers sometimes believe, happened before. It looks like destiny but is always the product of chance. It seems expected but is always unforeseen. This is why no psychoanalyst can claim to hold the key to reading the enigma of the encounter. Something always resists every reading, every interpretation.

The unknown of the encounter lies outside the world, beyond its laws. It does not allow itself to be deciphered. It falls in the order of the miraculous, the event, the advent. It is pointless to evoke those fantasies of the past, to call mothers and fathers to task, to even classify the qualities of the beloved. Rather, when we attempt the last there is always something on that list that leaves us dissatisfied. This list is never complete, it is never as we would like it to be, it is unable to explain the unknown of love. The loving encounter, when it exists, is a contingency that always exceeds everything that has gone before it, everything else that has happened. This is precisely why the encounter always carries within it the collision with alterity, with the obscurity of the Other.

'Amur'

We cannot choose who we love just as we cannot choose whether or not we are mad. As Lacan once said, 'one cannot choose to go mad'. 'I' cannot choose who to love. Falling in love, like madness, is not an act of will. Love and madness defy the powers of consciousness. The choice of the beloved does not come from the I, but from the unconscious. It responds to a collection of threads, details, plots, obscure reasons over which we have no control. When I say, 'I love you', Lacan reminds us, I must always add 'even if I don't really know why'. Love is never the result of a calculation. It isn't love because of a collection of qualities that would define the beloved. When we love we don't just love a part of the Other. Partial love cannot exist. Love demands love for the Other exactly as they are, and not for the Other that fits with the idealized representation of ourselves, not for the mirror of the Other. The loving encounter does not occur as a narcissistic mirroring, but as a smashing of the mirror, as an experience of an Other that is not like me, that differs from my I, from an I that I am not. The loving encounter, Lacan would say, is always the encounter with an *amur*,[5] with something that maintains its alterity like a wall (in French *mur*, with *amur* coming from the combination of the French word for love – *amour* – and that for wall, *mur*), something that we cannot possess, surpass or assimilate. In the Other we always love not that which is similar to us, but the *amur*. It is this divergence – the divergence of the *amur*, this residue – that can make the beloved truly irreplaceable, loved for each of their details. Desired, wanted, loved not for something but for everything. In this sense, as Lacan reminds us once more, love is never love for one of the beloved's qualities, but for their name. It is 'love for the Name', in which 'Name' stands for 'everything', for everything that the Other is in their alterity.[6] Love is not empathetic, it is not identification, not unification, but love for alterity. Love not for what is similar but for what is not, not for the same but for the different. It is precisely because of this that every declaration of love is made to something indecipherable, an unfathomable mystery:

> I do not love you as if you were salt-rose, or topaz,
> or the arrow of carnations the fire shoots off.
> I love you as certain dark things are to be loved,
> in secret, between the shadow and the soul.

The Promise

I love you as the plant that never blooms
but carries in itself the light of hidden flowers;
thanks to your love a certain solid fragrance,
risen from the earth, lives darkly in my body.

I love you without knowing how, or when, or from where.
I love you straightforwardly, without complexities or pride;
so I love you because I know no other way

than this: where I does not exist, nor you,
so close that your hand on my chest is my hand,
so close that your eyes close as I fall asleep.[7]

The Light

As we have seen, the encounter always lies in the order of mystery. Lovers would like everything to have already been decided, for this encounter to be destined for infinite repetition, to be forever. The declaration of love would like to include the eternal. Just as partial love for something does not exist, there is no love that does not challenge the aleatory nature of time: there is no love that does not want to be forever. Every love wants never to finish, to endure infinitely. Lovers would like their encounter to be a matter of destiny and not simple causality, chance, something otherwise unforeseen. No, lovers would like theirs to be an encounter that has always been written in the stars. In this sense, the encounter is not only an encounter with an obscurity that fascinates us, but also an extraordinary experience of light:

Then I met Linda, and the sun rose.

I can't find a better way to express it. The sun rose in my life. At first, as dawn breaking on the horizon, almost as if to say, this is where you have to look. Then came the first rays of sunshine, everything became clearer, lighter, more alive, and I became happier and happier, and then it hung in the sky of my life and shone and shone and shone.[8]

A light adorns the world with a new dress, a light that makes the world begin all over again. The loving encounter changes the face of the world. The world is the same, yet at the same time, it is not the same world as before. The stage of love is no longer that of One but of Two: it is the extraordinary beauty of sharing the world that accompanies the loving encounter. The world viewed through the eyes of Two is no longer the same world seen through the eyes of One.

Being Expected

According to Sartre, the joy of love lies in being expected. Before this encounter our lives had no meaning. Thanks to the encounter, our life acquires meaning as it is 'chosen', 'selected', 'called', 'expected', wanted in its most base details; loved for all that it is.[9] This is the joy of love and its promise: to make me feel expected, chosen, wanted in my most particular detail. And yet the encounter, despite lovers' illusions, always happens by chance. It is not possible to plan loving encounters. There is no agency in loving encounters. The encounter is always surprising, it is always unexpected, it defies calculation, planning. Are there places where it is more likely to happen? Are there incubator-places, places that are ideal for a loving encounter? Some think of supermarkets, of department stores, others of places we travel to visit or where we socialize. But can we really stake somewhere out in the hope that the person we are waiting for will pass by? Or, more likely, must we admit that the expectation of love never has any chance of being expected? I feel expected, I feel I have been expected only when I have been able to encounter the person who loves me. The loving encounter is both expected – always expected – and impossible to expect. We do not know where, how or when to expect it. We don't even know if it will ever happen. The encounter is akin to what mathematicians call a variable: it won't allow itself to be deciphered or manipulated, defying determination. Its joy, however, is unquestionable: the loving encounter saves my life from meaninglessness, from non-sense. It brings it meaning, it gives it meaning, it makes it feel unique and irreplaceable: in a word, expected.

Forever

Lovers dream of the encounter and believe it to be a sign of destiny, when in reality (as we have seen) the encounter happens by chance. It is pure contingency. I wasn't supposed to be there, I didn't have to go that way: the encounter is an unpredicted apparition. It is something that, when it happens, upends the rule shared by the canonical order of the world. The event of the encounter always belongs to the extraordinary order of the miraculous, of that which interrupts the smooth passing of time. And yet, every encounter always happens by chance. It is the result of a banal contingency: if I hadn't gone to that party, if I hadn't missed that train, I would never have met you. However, lovers dream of, and make a concerted effort to transform this causality, this pure contingency, into, destiny, a necessity. 'It was already written in the stars! I don't know how, or when, but this encounter had already been decided!', thinks the lover. It had already been decided that we would meet. Plato's myth of the androgynes, as told by Aristophanes, corroborates this illusion: the two halves are complementary, to love is to recreate the original whole, to literally find one's other half. This is the illusion of being and making a whole, of constructing a totality.

It is a fact. The loving encounter pushes lovers to not settle for the contingency of the encounter, pushing them towards its repetition. It pushes them towards contingency's translation into necessity, chance into destiny,[10] it pushes them to want it to be forever. Love does not settle for the instantaneous – to burn is not enough – love wants to last. This is why we have marriage and astrologers: to declare – using the symbolic Law of a pact or by making reference to the heavens – that it will be forever. With the encounter emerges the promise of sharing our own lives. It is the heartrending beauty of love that becomes solid, that knows how to last. This is why Odysseus in the *Odyssey* decides to carve his marital bed from an olive tree. Time does not conquer love. This is the test used by Penelope upon his return in order to confirm his identity. She wants to be certain that her man has not forgotten his promise but has stayed faithful to it, she wants a sign that his love has endured over time:

'Yet come, Eurycleia, strew for him the stout bedstead outside the well-built bridal chamber which he made himself. Thither do ye bring for him the stout bedstead, and cast upon it bedding, fleeces and cloaks and bright coverlets.' [. . .]

'Woman, truly this is a bitter word that thou hast spoken. Who has set my bed elsewhere? Hard would it be for one, though never so skilled, unless a god himself should come and easily by his will set it in another place.

But of men there is no mortal that lives, be he never so young and strong, who could easily pry it from its place, for a great token is wrought in the fashioned bed, and it was I that built it and none other.

A bush of long-leafed olive was growing within the court, strong and vigorous, and in girth it was like a pillar. Round about this I built my chamber, till I had finished it, with close-set stones, and I roofed it over well, and added to it jointed doors, close-fitting.

Thereafter I cut away the leafy branches of the long-leafed olive, and, trimming the trunk from the root, I smoothed it around with the adze well and cunningly, and made it straight to the line, thus fashioning the bed-post; and I bored it all with the augur.'[11]

Love is not a bed that can be unmade or abandoned, moved or changed. Odysseus carves their nuptial bed from a tree. He chooses an olive tree, a tree that grows slowly and lives a long life, a tree that knows the mystery of endurance. His bed is an image of the solid force of his love, of his faithfulness to the promise. This is why he is able to renounce the immortality offered by the goddess-nymph Calypso in order to return home and find his woman once more.

This is the folly of love when it exists: a lover's bed should always take the shape of the tree. 'Forever' is the expression that inhabits every loving discourse worthy of this name. 'Forever' is the attempt made by every love to give meaning to its own pure, inane causality as part of a manifestation of the eternal. It is the attempt to infinitely translate the contingency of the encounter into the need for the promise. Love happens by chance, but lovers are driven to make it eternal. Love worthy of its name demands endurance, it demands faithfulness to the promise. Lovers cannot settle for the instant that fatally passes into nothing. Love wants to endure, it wants the eternal, it wants to be 'forever'. This is the lovers' promise. The encounter causes the promise. The lovers who have met by chance want chance to reveal itself as fate. Will it burn again? Will it last? Will it endure even when it no longer burns?

Desire

The Fire of Sexual Desire

So-called scientific psychology reduces the kiss to nothing more than a way of ascertaining a partner's hygiene, a necessity to protect one's health. In the same way, it reduces loving ecstasy to the effects of dopamine on certain areas of the brain, destined to run their course within a rather short space of time, somewhere between ten and eighteen months. After this, a decision must be made: accept the decline in the erotic urge of desire or change partners in order to renew this act of cerebral doping with a new dose of dopamine.

If we look at the root of things, we see how desire is experienced much like a fire catching light. And there is no love that isn't accompanied by the fire of sexual desire. The protagonist of Philip Roth's novel *The Dying Animal* gives us no reason to doubt this. Sexual desire is the sole truth of the loving discourse. The encounter offers no enchantment that cannot be reduced to mere 'sexual interest':

Sex is all the enchantment required. Do men find women so enchanting once the sex is taken out? Does anyone find anyone of any sex that enchanting unless they have sexual business with them?[1]

We can even find this theme in the work of a great philosopher like Schopenhauer. In the chapter 'Metaphysics of Sexual Love', Schopenhauer (like the protagonist in Roth's book) has no doubt of love's subordination to the urgent needs of sexual instinct. Indeed, in his reflection he cynically reduces love to an 'illusion of instinct' bent unwittingly to the universal needs of the reproduction of the species. In other words, love is nothing more than a moral alibi for the impetuous and hyper-individual nature of the will to life and the sexual mechanics that manifests it.[2]

It would be brutally schematic to reduce the erotic current of desire to the manifestation of sexuality as pure will to life. The sexual instinct knows no eroticism, concerned exclusively as it is with the reproduction of the species. This is why Freud, when defining the sexual dimension of human life, rather than using the term instinct, used the term drive. In the animal world, which is dominated by instinct, there is no experience of eroticism. Nevertheless, eroticism does not coincide in any way with love. Eroticism is a component of human desire, but it is often precisely the loving attachment, the bond of love that endures but no longer burns, that extinguishes its impulse.

Sexual desire is never entirely in thrall to the law of sexual reproduction. Rather, this desire always appears as eccentric and deviant when we attempt to reduce sexuality to the framework of natural instincts. While instinct (which defines sexual orientation in the animal world) is inherited phylogenetically and coincides with the vital processes of the organism, the drive is an activity whose foundations lie in the perversion of natural instinct. It is one of Freud's greatest theoretical victories: the sex drive operates unburdened by the instinctive pressure of the reproduction of the species. It does not aim to subordinate sexuality to a finality of instinct, but demonstrates all of its deviance and lustful excess. The aim that propels the sex drive is not the reproduction of the species, but the perverse and polymorphic enjoyment of the body.

This is a framework of eroticism that does not belong in the animal world. It defines the dimension of sexual desire in human life. It is like a spring breeze, summer rain, an anarchic vital force that is not governed by the compass of instinct. It carries with it a lust that knows no law. In this sense, Lacan refers to a montage of drives and compares it to surrealist collages to underline the extraneous nature of sexual drive in the schematic linearity of instinct. This is the poetic, moving side of the sexual and erotic human body:

> They lie still, breathing softly, their heads on the long bolster still enclosed in its flowered case. The shutters are drawn. Noon has fallen. There is a faint clatter of plates and beyond that, a ritual silence. A radio, perhaps. An occasional car. They sleep. They awake in a different world. Dean's eyes drift about vaguely, finally falling upon the clock. An hour has passed. He sits up and quietly begins to remove his clothes, shoes first, then socks. The floor is cool and pleasant beneath his feet. They pose naked before the mirror. Dean is taller. His body is dark. He stands a bit to the side,

like her shadow. The light enters in thin, level strips, gills, which cross the floor. He slips his prick between her legs from behind and she gives it a little hug. She reaches behind her to stroke his balls with her fingertips. He looks like a lifeguard. There is a small roll of fat, a marble bannister, perched on his hip.

They make love slowly. He fixes her across the dark flowers and works it in as if fixing a log. Then he has her sit astride him. Her voice is invisible, a whisper from the street. 'It feels as if it's touching my heart,' she says. She raises herself slightly, her hands on his waist. 'I think it is,' she says. Dean smiles. He forces her down a bit. She struggles softly. Then he turns her over and sounds her. It's like a rain of love. Everywhere his mind turns he is drenched by it. As if in separate rooms, as if engaged in separate acts, they occupy themselves until the last instant and afterwards lie collapsed, the bedclothes scattered about them. Their voices are low, inconsequential. Outside the window, pigeons lurch across the tiles.[3]

Desire and Love

Does love's 'firm desire to endure', to borrow an expression from Paul Éluard,[4] the loyalty to the promise raised by the loving encounter, not perhaps clash with sexual desire's need to constantly renew its object? To 'burn' and therefore to exclude 'lasting'? It is Freud's belief that it is desire's destiny in a love life to divide itself between tenderness for one's partner and sexual desire for new lovers. He believes that the relationship between the intensity of desire and the length of the relationship is inversely proportionate. If love wants to endure, desire, on the contrary, wants to change partners in order to continue to desire. But isn't it impossible therefore to reconcile desire and love so they are not opposing? Where does the impossibility of this reconciliation come from? Is the result of desire's structural restlessness necessarily either resignation or infidelity? As neuroscience tells us, the brain is in continual need of renewing the sources that arouse desire. Woody Allen brought the mechanical dimension of desire to the screen in a compelling way, in his 1972 film, *Everything You Always Wanted to Know About Sex* (*But Were Afraid to Ask)*: sexuality is reduced to a movement of pistons, levers and pulleys set in action by central nervous systems governed by commands from the brain.

However, the sexual mechanics of desire do not obey the laws of nature. They are entirely surrealist and in no way realist. As such, sexual desire is never animal. This is its perverse, unnatural nature. There is no sexual norm for human beings. This is the ordinary lust that accompanies human sex lives, which are always eccentric when compared to any form of instinctive rules. It is a sexuality that is entirely uncoupled from the reproductive aims of instinct. Human beings are such because they are always at odds with the laws of nature.

Eroticism and Fetishism

Fetishism is the most resounding example of the unnatural nature of the sex drive. When I say 'I desire you', what am I saying? I desire your breasts or your shoes, your underwear or your legs? No human desire is free from fetishistic passion, especially in male sexuality. Fetishistic desire is, as such, deaf to love. The subject in its irreplaceable particularity, its Name, does not count: only the sexually irresistible presence of an object (the fetish) that can be localized in a part of the beloved's body matters. It is not the subject that counts but, as one of my patients who was permanently occupied with the act of seduction declared, the 'piece'. Here we can see a clear opposition between love that loves 'all' of the Other, or, as we have seen, their own Name, and the object's fetishistic passion as a passion for a part of the Other's body. While love is satiated by the sign of love, in the words of love, by love for the Name, desire is satiated by the foot or the shoe, by the body's details:

> I watch transfixed the girl who plays with the ends of her hair while ostensibly she is studying her History – while I am ostensibly studying mine. Another girl, wholly bland tucked in her classroom chair just the day before, will begin to swing her leg beneath the library table where she idly leafs through a Look magazine, and my craving knows no bounds. A third girl leans forward over her notebook, and with a muffled groan, as though I am being impaled, I observe the breasts beneath her blouse push softly into her folded arms. How I wish I were in those arms! Yes, almost nothing is necessary to set me in pursuit of a perfect stranger, nothing, say, but the knowledge that while taking notes from the encyclopaedia with her right hand, she cannot keep the index finger of her left hand from tracing circles on her lips. [. . .] 'Please,' they plead, 'why don't you just talk and be nice? You can be so nice, if you

want to be.' 'Yes, so they tell me.' 'But don't you see, this is only my body. I don't want to relate to you on that level.' 'You're out of luck. Nothing can be done about it. Your body is sensational.' 'Oh, don't start saying that again.' 'Your ass is sensational.' 'Please don't be crude. You don't talk that way in class. I love listening to you, but not when you insult me like this.' 'Insult? It's high praise. Your ass is marvellous. It's perfect. You should be thrilled to have it.' 'It's only what I sit on, David.' 'The hell it is. Ask a girl who doesn't own one quite that shape if she'd like to swap. That should bring you to your senses.' 'Please stop making fun of me and being sarcastic. Please.' 'I'm not making fun of you. I'm taking you as seriously as anyone has ever taken you in your life. Your ass is a masterpiece.'[5]

Here, Philip Roth outlines the difference between a feminine and a masculine way of loving. The feminine way uses the word, the sign of love, the exchange, the relationship. The masculine way instead reveals itself in its purely fetishistic idiocy, smashing the being of the Other into pieces, into detached fragments – the lips, the legs, the ass. Here we have an insurmountable antinomy that seems to undermine the stability of every loving relationship: the impossibility of reconciling love and the fetishistic nature of sexual desire. While love is satisfied by the sign of love, the words of love, the promise of love, by the 'forever' of the promise, while 'to love' means desiring everything of the Other, making them irreplaceable, the sexual desire that is satisfied by the foot, the shoe or, more precisely, by a 'piece' of the Other's body appears structurally unfaithful. While the loving relationship is between subject and subject, the fetishistic relationship is between a subject and an object. And the object, in this case, is susceptible to serial permutation.

The loving relationship thus finds itself immobilized by the permanent idiocy of the fetishism typical of masculine desire, which can seemingly never do without the 'piece'. But if masculine idiocy consists in rendering a detail of the beloved's body absolute, if sexual desire urges towards the fetishization of the body, reducing it to a 'piece', then feminine idiocy wears itself out through the repetition of the same question: 'Do you love me? Do you love me?' And no answer is ever enough to satisfy the perpetual nature of this question.

The demand for love does not demand the presence of the 'piece'. Instead it demands to be that which provokes lack in the Other. Feeling loved means feeling oneself to be the Other's lack, to be that which the Other is lacking. The fetishistic seriality of the piece thus finds itself replicated in the feminine iteration of love by the infinite nature of the demand for love. Lacan once described this difference between the demand for love that feeds the sign of desire in the Other and the sexual desire that feeds the presence of the fetishistic object using the paradox of Achilles and the tortoise, as formulated by the Eleatic philosopher Zeno. The two protagonists – Achilles and the tortoise – are destined never to meet, to always miss one another. The man searches for the object, the piece; the woman for the word, the sign of love. Love seen from the perspective of sexual desire is, therefore, a non-encounter, an illusion destined to end. This is why Lacan can state that 'the sexual relationship does not exist'.[6] What do you mean? Of course the sexual relationship exists! Actually, perhaps we should say, as the protagonist of Roth's novel *The Dying Animal* insists, that the sexual relationship is the only one that exists. And yet, no matter how many sexual relationships he is able to have, not one of them makes it possible to be and make One with the Other. The encounter between the tortoise and Achilles will never happen; one looks for the piece and finds the subject, the other looks for the subject and finds nothing more than an object.

So, what does this mean? Are poor Achilles and the poor tortoise destined to chase one another for all infinity without ever meeting? Sexual desire in itself cannot generate love. Rather it is love – the recognition of the irreplaceable nature of the beloved – that, when it unites with and is not separated from desire, can make the encounter between the Two possible.

When a Body Becomes a Book

The eroticization of the partner made possible by love is not only the eroticization of one part of the body, but the eroticization of the Other's very being, of their entire existence. It is no coincidence that the lover loves to take an interest in the beloved's entire life, where they came from, their origins, their memories, their childhood, their previous love and sex life, their inclinations, preferences, states of mind. The sexual encounter in itself is not a flash of lightning that burns out in the course of a night, but a secret that unites lovers. A break from the laws of the world – or if you prefer, from the wounds inflicted by life – that the Two allow one another to take.

> Sexual desire, when it is reciprocated, [. . .] is a conspiracy for two. The plan is to offer the other a break from the pain of the world. Not happiness, but physical respite from the enormous debt the body owes to pain [. . .] The conspiracy consists of creating a space together, a place of dispensation, and this dispensation, which is, by definition, only temporary, is from the immutable wound that the flesh has inherited. This place lies within the other's body. The conspiracy consists of losing oneself within this body, where everyone becomes impossible to find. Desire is an exchange of hiding places. (To reduce it to 'a desire to return to the womb' would be to trivialize it.)[7]

So, there is no regression, no return to the womb. The experience of sexual desire in love is the experience of a 'break from the pain of the world'. It is a time of beauty that is always able to suspend the time of the world. This means that the beloved's body can become a book, taking on the characteristics of a text, and we sense that reading that text is decisive, necessary, desired. It means that the Name itself can have the dignity of a body. We love the body and the life of the Other, treating them with the same dignity we would a book. I rummage around in the Other's body as if it were the pages of a favourite book. When love guides erotic desire, the life of the Other becomes a book. We would like to linger over it, dedicate time to it, experience the patience and beauty of reading. If the body becomes a book, there is no violence, no subjugation, no predation, there is only the search for the 'piece'. Reading a book is the opposite of a speedy appropriation, of a fragmentation of the body. We could say that this is the only real sexual education: to educate the subject to treat the body of the beloved as if it were a book and not just any old object to be consumed. The book, every book, distinguishes itself from a single object in the world, because it is a world itself.

3

Children

The son is a unique son. Not by number; each son of the father is
the unique son, the chosen son.

Emmanuel Lévinas, *Totality and Infinity*[1]

A Child Comes into the World

A child's arrival in the world changes it forever. A child is
nothing to the universal order of the world, it is like a blade
of grass in a field, a flower that appears on a stone wall, but it
is the blade of grass or the flower that forever changes the world
for parents. The birth of a child articulates a second birth of
the world, like the loving encounter between the Two. With
the birth of a child we experience once more the always-open
opening on the world.

The joy that accompanies the birth of a child multiplies the
love between the Two, opening it up to a new horizon. A child
is always generated by the Two and not the One, and in this
sense every child should be a metaphor for the love between
the Two. This means that a child carries with them the story
that has borne them, with the parents' desire and the love that
has united them at the forefront. The child isn't the child of the

sperm or the uterus of those who brought them into the world, but of their desire. They breathe the love (or refusal) of the person who wanted them (or not) in the world. This is their first inheritance: to have been desired by their parents' desire, or not. Not that this constitutes destiny. The child, every child, always has the possibility of modifying the fate they have been dealt by their parents. They always carry with them the possibility of rewriting that which Others have written about them.

The way in which parents see the world is the most fundamental inheritance that they leave their child. Our gaze on the world is the first gift we give the child who comes to the world. And they will, indeed, see the world through our eyes:

Daughter mine.
For you I would have given all the gardens
of my kingdom, had I been queen,
right to the last rose, right to the last feather. My kingdom for
   you.

But I leave you huts and thorns, thick dust covering the whole
   stage such heavy heartbeats
Sewn-up eyelids all around. Fury in the peripheries of the species
And at the centre. Fury.

But don't you believe those who paint the human as a lame beast
   and this world as the ball at the end of a chain
Don't believe those who paint everything pitch black and bloody.
   They do it because it's easy to do.

We are just confused, believe me. But let's listen. Let's listen
again.

We are still able to love something. We still feel pity.

It's your turn now,
it's your turn to wash these crusts of living bark.
There is splendour. Do not be afraid.

Hello beautiful face, most great joy.
Love is your destiny. Always. Nothing more.
Nothing more. Nothing more.[2]

The innocent existence of the child does not ask us to give
them goods, belongings, an income. As Mariangela Gualtieri
writes, 'gardens of my kingdom' are not necessary. 'Huts and
thorns' and 'thick dust' or 'fury' can be enough. What must be
passed on to the child is the very sentiment of life, a sense of the
'splendour' of the world. This sentiment of life that protects the
splendour of the world can only be transmitted through proof
from the parents that they still feel it, that they love something,
that they 'feel pity'. This is necessary for the child's life more
than anything else: to know that the 'splendour' of the world
exists in everything. This is all that is needed, the poet whispers,
'nothing more'.

More than One

As parents, we mustn't simply view our child as a narcissistic extension of our I or our own fantastical expectations, but as the plurality of the world, its limitless beauty. It is true how Freud explains that the birth of a child always coincides with the rebirth of the parents' narcissism. The child is identified with the imaginary phallus of the couple, and the parents' expectations, plans, fantasies all weigh on their shoulders. This is why the greatest gift a father or a mother can give a child is to abandon them, to let them take their own path. This is the particular nature of the family bond: it must be able to safeguard the child's life, to protect it, take care of it, love it, but the ultimate aim of this bond must be its dissolution in order to allow the child to separate themselves and have their own desire. It would truly be a nightmare, Deleuze once said, to find ourselves making someone else's dream come true.

The family was one of the preferred targets of the critical thought that came out of 1968. The accusation levelled at it is that of being a disciplinary, repressive institution, or a bourgeois façade hiding the most immoral violence and lies. The place of an austere containment of life, of its normative domestication. Great authors have also discussed this, as we can see in Bergman's 1973 film *Scenes from a Marriage*, *Festen* (1998) by Lars Von Trier and *American Pastoral* by Roth, to name but a few. Literature and cinema have always paid close attention to dissecting the family bond, laying bare its hidden aberrations. The same thing happens with those irrepressible critics of psychoanalysis' supposed familism, as we see in Deleuze and Guattari's *Anti-Oedipus*[3] and their radical critique of the Oedipal understanding of the family, or in the anti-psychiatry of Laing and Cooper, in which the middle-class family is pinpointed as the cause of madness itself.

This grubby view of the family certainly cannot insist on being the only way in which family life should be understood, as it is unable to recognize the beauty in the multiple that the family can, at times, make extraordinarily possible. The family is not just the location for a behavioural disciplining of life, it is not only the location of the parents' reborn narcissism, not solely a theatre for conflicts and accusations, but it is also the place where the Two experience the vital beauty of the multiple, of the collective, of 'more than One'. This is the enthusiasm that can sometimes characterize family life: the love of Two that has generated a new multiplicity. As Lévinas writes,[4] the child smashes the closed compactness of the One beyond repair, it forces plurality, impact with the 'more than One' in a far more convincing way than any philosophical theory.

In this sense, the child is a radical name of the unconscious: I am no longer master in my own house. Their life imposes upon me a limitless responsibility that is without end, it knows no bounds. Their life forces the Two into another time, another world, another life. In this sense, the birth of a child always implies a decentralization in the parents' lives. It offers a different depth to the passing of time, reinforcing a future that transcends the life of the Two. Time is no longer our time, life is no longer that of the Two. The birth of a child is the place of splendour (the splendour of the beauty of the child), but it is also the inevitable announcement of the death of those who have created them: their arrival in the world brings with it my, our end.[5]

Sacrificing Ourselves for Our Children

During the time of the patriarchy, the birth of a child irreversibly sealed the couple's fate. The child's life constituted the main reason for maintaining the marital union, even if the love between the Two had run its course and had no possibility of renewal. The child often became the ultimate reason for the life of the couple that, without its presence, would most probably have separated. Particularly before the law in Italy provided the right to divorce, many couples remained under the same roof solely to ensure the child received the care of both parents, and to protect them from any eventual trauma linked to the parents' separation. The results of such a choice were and are, to my mind, still rather dubious. If the child becomes the only reason for an unhappy couple to stay together, they risk becoming a sort of small idol to whom one of the Two (or both) elects to sacrifice their own happiness. This is not a good position for the child or the parents. The family is transformed into an asphyxiating trap where each person makes the Other's freedom impossible.

Before the cultural revolution of 1968 it was women in particular who had to renounce their desire and their freedom in order to ensure care and protection for their children, even when the love for their partner had long since disappeared. The law that legitimated the right to divorce is not – as some chose to insist, and still do – a law against the family, but a law that has *protected desire from sacrifice*, that recognizes how important it is that the family is defined not by hate and reciprocal resentment, but by love and respect, defending the child's interests first and foremost.

If family life is the result of moral or legal obligation, it lacks the very meaning of its existence, that of transmitting the sentiment of life to the child, beginning with the substantially positive testimony of life together. The drama comes when (as often happens) the children become the battlefield for the accusations and conflicts experienced in the life of a couple. The child then goes from being a metaphor for the love between the Two to bait, a tool for revenge, an ally to be fought over, a burden to get rid of.

When the Two experience a serious, irreversible crisis, or an actual rupture, the problem of what to do with the children inevitably raises its head. This is an increasingly frequent test facing parents today: is it possible to remain parents, to share the responsibility for the care and education of the children, without there any longer being love between the Two? The condition for this to happen is that the parents (particularly the one of the Two who is forced to undergo the separation, in cases where it is not consensual) are able to mourn their relationship, that they are able to lose themselves as a couple in order to continue as parents. For this reason, we must always differentiate between the parental couple and the loving couple.

The limitless responsibility that the child brings must never be confused with the sacrifice, in the name of the children, of one's own right to love. It is never a good thing to amputate a part of oneself, to mutilate one's own life by offering it in sacrifice to those we love. Sacrifice is a term that has no place in the lexicon of love. The economy of sacrifice is one of compensation, reimbursement: I sacrifice myself in order to receive something in return. The economy of love, however, is pure donation.[6] No act of parental love should demand any reimbursement because it is satisfied by itself, by its very existence. A couple that decides to stay together purely for the good of the children is a couple without desire that risks causing the child to become a kind of little idol who dictates the sacrifice of love between the Two in their own name. If the bond between the Two is not fed on reciprocal desire, it cannot help the child to grow.

The point is that it is possible to be good-enough parents without any longer being a loving couple, because these are two separate functions. There are families in which, even if after various difficulties the parents no longer exist as a couple and no longer live together, they have found their own balance with which to guarantee the child the right to be just that. In these cases, the symbolic difference between the function of parent and that of woman or man has prevailed over the accusatory conflict that pits one against the other.

Libidinal Confiscation

The birth of a child is not only, however, the time in which the world is born a second time. It is not only the time of plurality that breaks the closed circle of the One. Very frequently (if not always) the birth of a child also causes a kind of libidinal confiscation, or at the very least, a redistribution of the libido that can be destabilizing for the life of the Two. This is the other side of the coin, and the more problematic one. A child is not only the repetition of the love of the Two, but it is also the intrusion of an other between the Two. This intrusion can, as we have seen, be a source of beauty, but it can also give rise to a new feeling of distance between the Two. The child grabs all the libido in circulation. Children can become the cause of an irreversible alteration of desire. It is a risk that contradicts the commonly held belief that a child's birth always consolidates the couple. Very often the exact opposite occurs: the birth of a child always carries with it the risk of a crisis in the world of the Two, as the reinforcement of the family environment, the family bond, inevitably implies a gradual reduction in the erotic urge of desire. One of the most basic conditions for erotic desire is the existence of a necessary dose of distance and mystery, whilst excessive intimacy carries with it the risk of alienating desire.

As such, children can unite but they can also separate. Usually this separation does not lead to the end of the couple, but it does often force the couple to be drastically redefined. The child, itself generated from desire, risks compromising the couple's desire. This is the paradox: the child emerges from the desire of the Two but can also contribute to its extinction. Becoming a mother or father implies a change in the man or woman's position that can cause desire to collapse. Why does this happen so frequently? In the eyes of a man, the woman who becomes a mother can no longer be the cause of his erotic desire, and in the eyes of a woman, a man who becomes a father can, in equal measure, inhibit that desire.

Here, erotic desire once more meets the prohibition from its infancy: it is forbidden to have sex with one's own parents. A kind of fantasmatic incestuousness is renewed (a mother and a father cannot be objects of desire because of the prohibition of incest) and can unconsciously extinguish or cool the desire between the Two. If one's partner is no longer man or woman but now mother or father, the prohibition of incest is unconsciously restored. In this case, the child does not unite but separates. This is something that we often see repeated: the birth of a child tends to alter the dialectic of desire in the couple. The woman who becomes mother can extinguish the man's desire because the mother is the primary location of the prohibition. At the same time, the child's presence can cause the mother's desire to fully consume that of the woman, cutting out the man. The fundamental object of desire is no longer the partner but the child. This is why the first task facing a mother is to not be all-mother, but rather to exist as a woman who desires beyond the existence of her own child.[7]

When things work well enough, this alteration in the dialectic of desire is temporary, it is not irreversible. We must never forget that a family bond that is good-enough aims to allow the child's separation from the family. It is therefore a particular kind of bond: a bond that is necessary in order to make separation possible. But this separation must also happen to the parents. What we call 'separation trauma' does not only affect the child who is removed from the breast, but also, and above all, the Other from whom the child is removed. In order to allow separation from her own child, a mother must not be fully sucked in to her role as a mother, she must never be all-mother. In this sense I will insist on saying that it is the woman, the woman's being that separates the mother from her child. Thanks to the woman, desire can rediscover its vitality and avoid being imprisoned by the child.

4

Betrayal and Forgiveness

> Let any one of you who is without sin be the first to throw
> a stone at her.
>
> John 8:7

Jealousy

The promise of love wants to be forever, but it is not possible for love's 'forever' to be guaranteed, ensured. The promise's fate is never already written, not in the stars, not in marriage contracts or religious vows. Despite what lovers might say, there is never a guarantee that a love will be 'forever'. The end of love, even the greatest love, is always possible. Deceit accompanies the vow of love like a shadow.

The anxieties related to jealousy reflect better than any other all love's inability to exclude its own death. Jealousy is indeed the sentiment that erupts in the life of the Two with the idea that the beloved prefers someone else. For the one who is jealous, the exclusive time of the Two – their hiding place – risks being forever traumatized by the eruption of a third outsider that expropriates one of the Two from the love of the Other, causing their loss. This is the reason why every love tends to be jealous. The presence of a threatening triangulation always lies at the basis of jealousy. But while female jealousy tends to structure itself around the fantasy of losing love, of being abandoned, of no longer feeling like the one and only for the Other, male jealousy tends to be projective, pouring suspicion of an urge to betray onto the beloved, an urge that actually belongs to the jealous subject. This is a fundamental lesson taught by clinical experience: the jealous man is generally the most unfaithful of men (consciously or unconsciously). It is his way of diverting what he experiences inside onto his partner, in order to shift his own guilt onto an external entity.

Jealousy does not, in general, limit itself to simply causing the subject to view every single thing through the prism of their own fantasy of betrayal (as happens to Shakespeare's Othello, influenced by the squalid Iago), but casts doubt over every aspect of their partner's life, past, present and future. *The jealous man experiences the anxiety-making, and in no way joyful, freedom of the beloved*. He experiences this freedom as if it were torture, like a constant prophecy of an imminent loss. Rather than experiencing love as absolute exposure to the absolute freedom of the Other, he would prefer to reduce his beloved to an object like all the others he possesses. This is the illusion of jealousy as illustrated by Proust:

> We imagine that it [love] has as its object a being that can be laid down in front of us, enclosed in a body. Alas, it is the extension of that being to all the points in space and time that it has occupied and will occupy. [. . .] But we cannot touch all these points.[1]

The urge to appropriate love would like to possess all the time (past, present and future) and occupied spaces of the beloved object. On one hand, the lover demands to know their beloved inside and out, but on the other, they are forced to recognize that there lies within the beloved a secret that makes them impenetrable, illegible, impossible to appropriate.

In the tale recounted by Alberto Moravia in *Boredom*, Cecilia's fundamental trait is that she is seen by the painter who loves her as 'elusive', but this is not revealed immediately. At the beginning of their relationship, Cecilia places herself at Dino's total disposal (sexually, in particular), as if she were an inanimate object. No loving passion is unleashed in her partner until he discovers that Cecilia has another man. She only acquires mystery when she reveals her freedom, when she demonstrates that her desire is not satisfied by the relationship with her painter lover. Cecilia's absence becomes unbearable because it is synonymous with her alterity, with the impossibility of his being able to possess her completely. And it is precisely this impossibility that provokes in Dino a morbid jealousy and imperious desire. And yet, 'however roughly I treated her, however much I squeezed her and bit her and penetrated her, I failed to possess Cecilia and she was elsewhere, God knows where'.[2] In this way, Dino must discover the aleatory nature of the 'male illusion that looks upon physical possession as the only real possession'.[3] The vain sexual frenzy that takes him over is destined to collide with an insurmountable truth: that no one can possess the absolute freedom of their beloved. In this sense, the Other is, by definition (and as is embodied perfectly by Cecilia), always 'elusive', or as Barthes would say, 'unqualifiable', 'atopic':[4]

> Significantly, the feeling that I had not truly possessed her generally used to assail me at the moment when, fully dressed, and saying goodbye to me, she walked toward the door in order to leave; it was as though her departure suddenly revealed to me, in an entirely physical manner, her unchanging power to withdraw herself from me, to elude me. Then I would pursue her, seize her by the hair and hurl her on the divan, disregarding her protests which in any case were not very energetic, and have her again, just as she was, fully dressed, with her shoes on her feet and her bag on her arm, still with the illusory idea that by having her I could nullify her independence and her mystery. Immediately after the embrace I realized, of course, that I had not possessed her.[5]

With the discovery of the betrayal, a new phase in their story begins. Dino sees Cecilia as 'mysterious' and 'elusive', leading him to attempt, in every possible way, to return her to that condition of the passive, inanimate object she was when they first met. His sexual frenzy intensifies, he tries showering her with money, he proposes marriage, he declares he will still love her even if she continues with her adulterous relationship. He even considers killing her in order to liberate himself from the pain and feelings of lack that Cecilia has brought to his life. But his efforts are all in vain. Cecilia refuses all of his proposals in order to preserve her own freedom. The laceration of his condition caused by love that is not fully reciprocated becomes unbearable for Dino, to the point where it leads him to commit the suicidal act of crashing his car into a tree.

At the heart of jealousy is the terror of being deprived of the beloved object, and consequently, the demand to ensure their absolute possession. As such, it is no coincidence that jealousy can lead to violent acts aimed at reiterating an exclusive ownership over the beloved. Jealous possession wants to suppress the impenetrable nature of the beloved, to limit their freedom until it is reduced to an object like any other over which the subject can exercise their unlimited dominion. But this is impossible.

Every Great Love Can Die

Lovers are surrounded by an uncomfortable truth: every love, even the greatest and most absolute, can die. Every love can prematurely come to an end, contradicting its own aspirations for eternity. Every love that swears fidelity can encounter its deceit, sooner or later meeting its own demise.

What in jealousy had remained at a fantasmatic level, in the form of a permanent fear of feeling betrayed, becomes a reality with betrayal. It is the profound truth of love that comes to light when we encounter the sharp edge of betrayal: not only has the person I loved betrayed their promise, but every promise, the very promise of love, the promise that it would be forever, reveals itself to be a promise that can only be experienced precariously, that cannot be ensured by any contract or any vow. So, the discovery of betrayal is very similar to what Jean Améry, the Austrian writer who took part in the Belgian resistance against the Nazi invasion describes when he was captured and tortured. He knew very well that he was risking his life with his political action. Rationally he knew this, just as he was well aware that, in the case of his capture, he would not be spared the violence of prison and torture in order to extract information from him. But this knowledge remained abstract. It was only after being tied to the chair by his captors and receiving that first blow that he truly encountered the truth of what he already knew:

> The first blow brings home to the prisoner that he is helpless, and thus it already contains in the bud everything that is to come. One may have known about torture and death in the cell [. . .] but upon the first blow they are anticipated as real possibilities, yes, as certainties. They are permitted to punch me in the face [. . .] they will do with me what they want. Whoever would rush to the prisoner's aid – a wife, a mother, a brother or friend – he won't get this far. [. . .] At the first blow, however, trust in the world breaks down.[6]

The first blow does not only violate the confines of the body, but causes his very faith in the world to crumble. In the hands of his tormentors, his most naked intimacy feels violated. He is plunged into the solitary experience of the fallen. No one can help him now. He has lost everything. That which up until the 'first blow' he knew only in a rational, abstract way is now an atrocious reality.

Doesn't something similar happen to the person in love when their trust is betrayed? Every lover is well aware that no love – their own included – can truly be 'forever', can be sure of its own promise. And yet the lover only discovers the bitterness of this truth when they experience the trauma of betrayal; when, as happens to Améry, bound to a chair, they receive that first hit, the first blow. In both cases, the sensation is that of being at a point of no return, of having lost everything. If at first the beloved's love gave meaning to the world, with the trauma of betrayal nothing is how it used to be: the world has been stripped of meaning. I have been abandoned. Not only is my trust in the person I loved broken, but my trust in the very world that was born as a result of our love.

The Atrocity of the Work of Forgiveness

Is it possible to forgive betrayal?[7] Is it possible for a love that has known lies, deceit, betrayal to return to how it was before? Forgiveness is an atrocious work. In some ways, it is similar to that of mourning. It requires the psychical digestion of a loss. The ideal image of the beloved has been destroyed forever. The vase has been smashed to pieces. And it is impossible to recover, for it to go back to how it was before. But, unlike the sorrowful work of mourning, the atrocious work of forgiveness implies that the object is not irreversibly dead. It is dead, but it is also still alive. It has gone, but is still here.

Can we forget a betrayal? Don't they say that time heals all wounds? Do we forget it because it grows weaker, because the memory of the trauma of betrayal is naturally extinguished? Because of memory loss? Does a sort of amnesia fall over the lover's wound, leaving that blow to be forgotten?

As with the work of mourning, forgiveness also revolves around the fall, the loss of a presence that gave meaning to the world and my existence. That presence no longer exists. It is the two-fold experience of the lack that features in every act of mourning: the world without that presence is emptied of meaning and my existence is as lost as the world.

Forgiveness can never be an immediate response to betrayal. It requires time, much like any work of mourning. There is no reactive forgiveness, in the same way that speedy or easy mourning does not exist. This is what is so atrocious about it: it requires time. Furthermore, the work of forgiveness, like that of mourning, does not cancel out the trauma of loss. It cannot cause it to be forgotten, it can only attempt to elaborate it symbolically once more. To forgive does not mean to forget: *one does not forgive because they forget, but they can only forget if they forgive.*

There is only one condition that allows the work of forgiveness to reach its completion: this is the *welcoming of the Other's imperfection* as representative of my own imperfection. It is possible to forgive out of love, but it is equally possible, with the same dignity, to not be able to forgive out of love. That which is unforgivable about the trauma of betrayal is not the betrayal of the body, but that betrayal of the pact and the word that the betrayal of the body implies. A love can always end, but betrayal does not necessarily mean the end of a love. On the contrary, if someone who betrays experiences their actions with anxiety it is because they would like to continue staying in love: someone who betrays, very often, loves the person they betray.

For this reason, the drama of betrayal can also involve the person who has betrayed if they are still in love. And forgiving oneself is perhaps even more difficult than forgiving the Other. In this sense, saying goodbye is less atrocious and painful than betrayal because, in betrayal, the person who breaks the pact asks that the love might continue to exist, that it might not die despite having mortally wounded it: they ask to go down that atrocious path of the work of forgiveness. It is only thanks to this work, which never truly ends (forgiveness, as Derrida reminds us on numerous occasions, is only such if it is capable of 'forgiving the unforgivable'[8]), that love's life can pick itself up and start again. With the necessary caveat that we are not masters of this work. Someone cannot decide to forgive. It is only the atrocious work of forgiveness that can bring about forgiveness; not as its outcome, but as a kind of supplementary gift, a kind of grace.

The Wound that Became Poetry

As happens with the difficult work of mourning, the work of forgiveness never manages to erase the open wound left by the trauma of betrayal. In mourning, this wound is caused by the loss of someone who is no longer with us. In forgiveness, the wound is caused by the loss of trust in the beloved's word. The scar left by betrayal remains etched on the lover's body.

Its presence is indelible. The vase cannot be like it was before it was broken. Forgiveness cannot erase the wound. Rather, when it happens, it transforms the wound, elevating it to the dignity of a poem.

There is an ancient Japanese art form that we can use to illustrate the miracle of forgiveness. It is called *Kintsugi*. It is surrounded by legend: a very powerful mandarin accidentally breaks a vase from his precious collection. Despairing, he searches for an artisan capable of putting the vase back together just as it had been originally. A man is recommended to him, and the mandarin entrusts the fragments of his precious vase to this elderly craftsman. However, rather than attempting to hide the flaws in the vase, to reconstruct it faithfully by concealing the cracks, the craftsman intentionally highlights them, painting them with gold. It is said that other mandarins who learnt of the devastating beauty of this vase purposefully smashed their own in order for them to be rebuilt in the same style.

With the art of *Kintsugi* we see an extraordinary operation in action: the vase is still the same one as before despite the fact that it is not. It has changed image, it is another vase, and yet it is built from the remnants of the broken one. Despite the trauma caused by its breakage, thanks to the knowing hands of the old artisan, this breakage provided the *opportunity for a new creation*. The cracks have been painted with gold; the scars have become poetry. In this sense, the experience of forgiveness is one of *resurrection*. The love that appeared to be dead, finished, hopelessly cast into the dirt, returns to life, starts over once more, begins again. Thanks to forgiveness, the loss and death of love are not the last word on love: forgiveness allows love to start again, just as it allows the life that was believed to be dead to be reborn. Forgiveness ensures that destruction and death are not the final words on life.

5

Violence

In effect, what it [sadism] seeks to appropriate is the victim's transcendent freedom. But it is just this freedom that remains necessarily out of reach. And the more the sadist insists on treating the other as an instrument, the more this freedom escapes him.

Jean-Paul Sartre, *Being and Nothingness*[1]

Hitler's Bitch

There are good things, and there are bad things, there are many more good things than bad. The good things happen every day, the bad things only at certain times of day and then they pass quickly and the good things return. One small good thing is scratching yourself. Like this (she scratches behind the ear). Or like this (she scratches her belly). One of the best things is the ball, chewing the ball, feeling the ball between your teeth, letting it fall from your mouth, picking the ball up between your teeth again, chewing, chewing the ball. Biscuits are also good things, smelling the biscuit, getting your snout next to the biscuit and then (slowly though, really slowly) taking the biscuit between your teeth, chewing the biscuit, feeling the biscuit breaking on your tongue, eating the biscuit. The other good thing about biscuits is that they give me one when I've been good, and after the biscuit they stroke my head, a biscuit and a caress, and as well as the caress there is another thing that is even better than the biscuit, there is one thing that is better than all the others (I'm going to tell them), there is one thing without which even the other good things aren't good any more (I'm going to tell them, I'm going to tell them), there is one thing that is the best of all the best things (now I'll tell them, I'll tell them, I'll tell them); the best thing of all is the master, the master, the master! [. . .] The master is the thing that makes all those things that are already good even better. [. . .] To follow the master, to smell his boots. My master has boots [. . .] The important thing is to have a master. To have a master with boots [. . .] is the best thing in the world![2]

The narrator here is Hitler's dog, Blondi. More precisely, Hitler's bitch. Is this perhaps every man's desire, his ideal love? To have as a partner an obedient, grovelling bitch? Hitler probably loved women who were similar to his dog, ready to do anything for him but never capable of having a real relationship with him. Is this a man's loving desire? It is beyond doubt that love, for men, is an experience that erodes their identity. Men tend to be undivided, uniform, compact. Man's phallic display exhibits a phallic prestige that excludes the lack, the wound, the fragility. Contrary to this, love introduces a lack into the very heart of the compact identity that the possession of the phallus would like to establish. By making man's relationship with his own lack more confidential, love renders man similar to woman. The beloved is not that which must fill a void (*'I love you because I miss you'*), but that which opens a void – *'I miss you because I love you.'* For this reason, Lacan declared that love, regardless of the form it may take (homosexual, heterosexual, lesbian, and so on), is always 'love for a woman', because of the absolute freedom of which woman is emblematic. Fetishism, like violence visited upon an other (which is on an entirely different level, and far worse) is one of the male ways of exorcising the uncontrollable anarchy of woman. In Tornatore's 2013 film *The Best Offer*, a man reduces the irreducible anarchy of woman to a series of paintings that he contemplates ecstatically from a bunker in his house. It is better to possess the image of woman than to be confronted with a real woman. Images, explained a patient of mine who was a compulsive masturbator, do not speak, I can do what I want with them. This is a kind of retinoic fetishism: choosing a part of a body or object to take the place of the freedom, the anarchy, the singularity of woman.

But does the urge to appropriate belong to all love? Not just to sick love, but to the loving desire that wants the beloved not to go away, to remain forever his? If love provides respite from the pain in the world, then we would never want to lose the unique opportunity that it offers us. We desire to lose ourselves in the person we love, to feel our heart in theirs, to lose ourselves in them. For this reason, to love is never to love something of the Other but 'everything'; to love 'all' of the Other, each of their most minuscule details, each of their imperfections, each of their symptoms. At the same time, however, no love will ever be able to make or be an 'all' with the Other. *Love loves everything about the Other, but cannot do everything with the Other.* The absolute alterity of the Other forbids the Two from ever making One. Every love is obliged to experience always being 'not-all' because in its experience it must encounter the impossibility of unification and harmony. This is not, however, a limit, a catch, a trap. It is the miraculous beauty of love: to love everything about the Other without ever making an all with the Other; being attracted by its mystery, by its secret, by its alterity, which can never be ours.

This is why Lacan maintained (in a way that might, at first glance, seem hermetic) that *when we love we always love a woman.* What does this mean? Well, if 'woman' is the name of *heteros*, of alterity, of the impenetrability or impossibility of possessing the Other, then to love is always to love a 'woman', to love that which is *heteros*. This means, to cite another of Lacan's aphorisms, that love is always 'heterosexual' because there is no love that is not a love for that which is *heteros*. This 'hetero-sexuality' is obviously non-anatomical, but is such because it exposes us to the encounter with the inassimilable difference of the Other. This is why love excludes the homogeneous, the *homo*, appearance and identity.

Lesbian or homosexual love, like so-called heterosexual love, can only be love if there is a love for the *heteros*. In other words: if there is heterosexual love not in the anatomical sense, but in a profoundly ethical sense – love for a 'woman'. Love is always heterosexual because either it is love for that which is *heteros* in its alterity, or it is not love. Love is always love for a 'woman' as woman embodies the experience of non-homogeneity, the non-identical, of difference, in the most radical way possible.

The consequence of this premise is the fact that love is always a risky exposure to the irreducible freedom of the Other. Love is not possible if there is not complete trust in an Other that I know I can never truly know, that I know to be *heteros*, different from me and impossible to possess.

Freedom and Ownership

And yet love always implies a desire to appropriate. This does not mean simply possessing the beloved's body. It does not mean imprisoning, possessing the freedom of the beloved so that it is only mine, as Proust's protagonist in *In Search of Lost Time* or that of Moravia's *Boredom* attempt to do. The design that accompanies every love is much more subtle: I do not want the beloved's possession to exclude their freedom, I do not want to obtain their absolute fidelity by limiting their freedom, as happens with Proust's protagonist who forces Albertine to live locked in her own house. The lover's ambition is different: they desire the other to be faithful, to be only theirs, but as the result of an entirely free choice and not through some form of coercion. This is the dream of every person in love: to possess the beloved's freedom because it is free. To possess their freedom, leaving them free. But as Sartre rightly asked as he reflected on this paradox intrinsic to every love, how can a 'captive freedom' exist? Isn't this a clear contradiction in terms?[3]

When I possess my love as if it were a thing, my desire is destined to be extinguished and my love itself to perish because I do not solely desire the body of the beloved, I don't desire to own them absolutely only as a result of coercion. The paradox is that if I stop my beloved from being free, I mutilate my own loving desire, which can only exist thanks to the Other's freedom. This is the first hurdle. As we have seen, Alberto Moravia in *Boredom* illustrates this with precision, demonstrating how it is only through her absence, her being elsewhere, her betrayal, that Cecilia truly acquires the value of a loving and erotic object in Dino's eyes. When Cecilia is entirely at his disposal, present, when she is his property, boredom sets in:

> Strange to say, no sooner had I given shape to these reflections than the figure of Cecilia, which, as long as I had suspected her of betraying me, had been living and real to me, although mysterious (in fact, precisely because mysterious) – now that I was doubtful about her betrayal, became unreal and boring again as in the past.[4]

The crossroads at which Moravia's protagonist finds himself is the same one that often emerges in love. On the one hand, there is a possession that clips the wings of desire because desire needs to grasp the Other not as an object at their full disposal, but as a true subject. On the other hand, however, if I take this path, the one which attributes the dignity of a wholly free subject to my beloved, if I therefore renounce any plans to appropriate, if, as the dignity of love requests, I attempt to disarm myself before the Other's freedom, I am fatally forced to experience their irreducible nature, the fact that they cannot be appropriated. This is the second hurdle: I cannot buy, imprison, possess the freedom of the *heteros*, I can only love it in all its alterity. However, loving it means fully understanding its unreachable, elusive character, as happens in the paradox of Achilles and the tortoise.

In other words, any attempt to possess freedom as freedom always leads to stalemate. So, I must experience the absolute impossibility of penetrating, assimilating the Other, I must experience their unreachable secret. This is why for Proust the essence of the beloved woman is always a 'fugitive', even when we hold them tight in our arms. In short, an essence that can never, by its very nature, be 'ours':

> such persons are fugitives. To understand the emotions which they arouse, and which others, even better looking, do not, we must recognise that they are not immobile, but in motion, and add to their person a sign which corresponds to that which in physics denotes speed.[5]

The fact that Proust defines the loved being as being in movement clearly demonstrates the risk implied by every love. If the beloved is immobile in their body when it is in my arms, this immobility is only an appearance, because even when they are in my arms (as Proust rightly reminds us) their essence is elsewhere. I can never take possession of their absolute freedom. This is the paradox that Barthes describes brilliantly with the example of the child who takes apart an alarm clock in order to discover the secret of time:

> I am searching the other's body as if I wanted to see what was inside it, as if the mechanical cause of my desire were in the adverse body (I am like those children who take a clock apart to find out what time is).[6]

It is not, therefore, so certain that those who lament being without love truly desire to expose their lives to the risk that the impact with this irreducible alterity implies. This is particularly true of men for whom the loving encounter is an experience that fatally erodes their identity. This is why Barthes was able to write that love always implies a certain 'miraculous' amount of 'feminization' in every man.[7] It is, in fact, this falling in love that makes a man similar to a woman, and therefore more exposed to the risk of love, to loss and lack, unencumbered by the phallus. Love is always female: it is always love for a 'woman', for the absolute freedom of which woman is emblematic.

Violence as a Profanation of Love

The violence that aims to reduce the Other to an object in our hands has nothing to do with love and is merely its pathological distortion, or rather, its profanation. If the loving experience confronts us with the desire to keep the person we love with us, to feel them ours, to share the unshareable dimension of their freedom, it is because, in reality, every lover knows that the enchantment of love can always end, that nowhere is it written in the stars that it will be forever. In this sense also, love implies taking a significant risk. The experience of love always undermines our own identity, leaving us lacking. It destabilizes our self-sufficiency, leaving us dependent on the Other: *I don't love you because I miss you, but I miss you because I love you.*

The use of violence can be a desperate attempt to avoid the risk of loss and the end that every love carries with it, forcing a kind of unbreakable bond on the beloved. The violence of appropriation would prefer to transform the woman into a lifeless object than be exposed to the risk of losing her. Rather than confronting myself with the absolute freedom of the Other, I prefer to become absolute master of that freedom. I want to make the beloved 'my thing', as Giovanni Verga's Mastro don Gesualdo would say, to put her in a 'drawer' as Molière's Miser might like to do. This is a typically male attitude with its cultural foundations in the patriarchal ideology that believed woman to have only one destiny, or rather, that there was only one way for her to atone for her intrinsic sinfulness: to become a mother. This is the well-known patriarchal opposition between woman-as-Eve (a source of temptation and destruction) and the mother-as-the-Virgin-Mary (the source of all that is good) that inspired the necessary and terrifying use of fire, theorized by the Dominicans in the *Malleus Maleficarum* ('The Hammer of Witches', 1487), as a tool for the torture, penance, purification and final redemption of woman from the obscene power of the devil that possesses her. At the forefront of this scene, that of the physical elimination of witches, is a representation of woman that is not only sexuophobic, but misogynistic. The witch appeared as the symbol of the anarchic and indomitable nature (the *heteros* nature) of femininity that refuses to passively adhere to the patriarchal representation of woman as the keeper of the home and attentive mother to her own children. According to that culture, only through self-sacrifice, through the sacrifice of her freedom and desires, could a woman redeem her own sinful and tempting ways and the innate weakness of her intellect (embodied by the biblical figure of Eve), masochistically devoting herself to the role of child-bearer and the obedient servant of the family.

In patriarchal ideology, the woman who is not all-mother is a whore: Eve the sinner versus the Virgin Mary. However, women's bodies are nothing more than a false target on which male chauvinist violence is unleashed. The real aim of this violence is actually to impair and strike woman's freedom, to transform the woman into Hitler's bitch. Freedom is, indeed, synonymous with alterity and it is that which the patriarchal culture has tried in all possible ways to eradicate from the body of woman.

This appears with dramatic force in a pivotal scene of Elena Ferrante's *My Brilliant Friend*, with the act of a boy who literally tries to rip out Lila's tongue because she refuses to obey his commands. Saverio Costanzo's recent television adaptation emphasizes this scene beyond the space it is given in Ferrante's text. Lila's unforgivable error is that of having humiliated the boy's younger brother at school by proving herself to be much better prepared than him. The tongue therefore becomes an essential metaphor of woman's freedom. Silencing Lila by ripping out her tongue (or sticking it with a pin as it is in the text[8]) means wanting to deprive the Other of their freedom, subjecting the woman to the male power. In this case, the use of violence by the boy marries perfectly with the sadism wielded to defend his wounded male pride.

The Refusal of Femininity

In this literary episode, as with numerous news stories up to and including openly criminal acts of femicide, it is clear how male chauvinist violence wants to burn the residue that woman's freedom introduces to every attempt to appropriate it. This violence reacts to the anxiety felt when faced with this freedom without guarantees embodied by every woman. Women can also kill, harass and hate out of love. When this happens, it is as if they have become trapped in the mirage of violence that confuses love with the right to appropriate the Other's freedom, as if in an optical illusion.

This means that the difficulty of loving the difference, of loving the Other as an incarnation of that which is *heteros*, is a difficulty that can also be found in women. It is no coincidence that Freud spoke of the 'rejection of femininity',[9] of the woman's *heteros* (which obviously has nothing to do with her lack of a penis) as a problem common to both sexes. The rejection of femininity means not being able to bear the alterity of the freedom embodied by woman. In a man this means rejecting the woman as a place of lack, of dis-identity, of their own castration. But what does the rejection of femininity mean for a woman?

If a woman is the one to erode identity, if the woman is (as we have seen) the most proper name of freedom, if (as Lacan would say) Woman does not exist,[10] if the Woman's identity does not exist then every woman, one by one, is obliged to invent her own female identity against the background of her universal non-existence. In other words, if the Woman is not a valid norm with which all women can identify, if this norm – the normality of woman – does not exist, then every woman must face the difficult task of being woman in her own way.

Whilst the phallic identity is a uniform that works for all men, such a uniform does not exist for women. Each woman is an exception, each woman is unique, each woman invents her own way of being a woman. Whilst the male inherits the hallmarks of virility (of his phallic identity) from his father, this is not possible for a woman as not even her mother knows what it means to be a woman. This is the reason for the often vindictive, furiously ambivalent disposition that can characterize the mother–daughter relationship: the daughter can direct her aggression towards her mother, who is guilty of not being able to answer the question: 'What does it mean to be a woman?'

No woman truly knows what it means to be a woman. It is in this not-knowing that male violence is able to intervene, as, paradoxically, it always carries with it a kind of pedagogical vocation: it wants to explain to a woman what it means to be a woman. But if a woman is unable to answer this question, then there is no chance of a man being capable. Some women fall into the trap of seeing the man as an infallible compass capable of guiding them towards being a woman. This is a very dangerous illusion that can lead a masochistic inclination towards a man-as-master: to be subjected to violence and receive in return the answer to the question: 'What does it mean to be a woman?', searching for the way to guide one's own freedom without it causing anxiety in a man – 'How can I become a real woman?' – to the point of making oneself the (masochistic) object of male violence and to embody the fetishistic object of the male fantasy, indulging his every will, much like Hitler's bitch.

This is why man often tends to perversely portray himself as the person who can educate the woman in the ways of obedience. The violent man always hides a sadistic pedagogue: he would like to explain to the woman how she should love and how love coincides with the rejection of the self, with one's own enslavement, with the addition that one of the manifestations of woman's freedom involves the enjoyment of her body. Indeed, there is a clear divergence between the feminine way of enjoying and the male way. Male enjoyment is hegemonized by the monarchy of the phallus; it is an obvious, exterior enjoyment, defined by the orgasm and the successive detumescence of the organ. Its mechanism is hydraulic. Female enjoyment is not obvious (a woman, unlike a man, can lie about her orgasm and her pleasure), it is not colonized by the phallus and does not respond in any way to a hydraulic mechanism. Female enjoyment removes itself from the monarchy of the phallus in order to scatter itself over the whole surface of the body. This enjoyment is anarchic, boundless, without limit; the orgasm does not extinguish it, but can set it burning once more. It is an enjoyment that Freud would have defined as 'oceanic'. Faced with this bottomless enjoyment every man has a sense of inadequacy and impotence. In order to preserve his own power and exorcise the abyss of female enjoyment (which not only scares men but also women), men can identify the woman as a whore. The affirmation 'they are all whores' is, in fact, a common way of attempting to isolate female enjoyment.

Another unnerving aspect of violence against women is how it is possible for women subjected to male violence to remain firmly attached to it, rather than resolutely detaching themselves from the flame that burns them. This does not depend solely on the pervasive nature of patriarchal ideology in culture. I have analysed many emancipated women who experienced this condition with a sense of profound confusion. We can perhaps explain this enigma by making reference to the Freudian category of 'rejection of femininity'. There are women who get used to violence because when faced with the seemingly impossible problem of their feminine identity ('What does it mean to be a woman?') they tend to make the man (who actually knows absolutely nothing about the mystery of woman) their sadistic master, thus delivering into the man's hands the responsibility of solving this problem. The result is submission to the man who creates suffering, and at the same time, a frustrating sense of dependency. The result is that of delivering one's own life into the sadistic hands that, rather than nurturing love, kill it:

'Good girl Blondi,' sounds the master, and he gets closer, closer. My master. The best thing in the world, closer, closer (my master, my dear dear master) and something in his hands that is not a biscuit, is not a ball, goes crack. [. . .] It is not biscuit. They close my mouth, strong hands. He looks at me, the master, but I can't see him any more . . . Blondi sees only Blondi . . .[11]

6

Separations

Indifference and Deceit

Every promise, including the promise of love, contains ambiguity: as Derrida reminds us, every vow carries with it the long shadow of deceit. Not because of a lack of faith, but because of the inexorable nature of things. Someone who promises today that the love that binds them to the Other will last forever will no longer be the same person who made that vow after just a few months. So, the pact between lovers – beyond the stars and marriage contracts – demands that faithfulness to that 'forever', to the promise, be renewed each day, as every love that wants to last forever can always, at any moment, meet its end. Every love, despite wanting to be eternal, walks the taut, narrow tightrope between appearance and disappearance, life and death.

Why then, as Barthes rightly asks, is it better to last than to burn? Wouldn't it be better to burn without pointlessly turning to the illusion of endurance? Isn't this the temptation that defines our time? Desire either burns or it lasts without life. There is no option for love to last as it burns. Lasting and burning exclude one another: if it burns it doesn't last, and if it lasts it doesn't burn.

Every loving relationship hangs in the balance. It is not, as common sense would have it, making and being One with the Other: love is never an 'all'. I love everything about the Other, but love is always a not-all, excluding correlation, fusion or permeation. It was Plato who, using the discourse of Aristophanes in the *Symposium*, generated the illusion of spherical love, love as the recomposition of the whole, as One. The myth of Eros recounted by Aristophanes highlights three phases in the genesis of this illusion. First, there would have been androgynous beings, cylindrical hermaphrodites who possessed both sets of genitals. Their self-sufficiency and their arrogance led them to attack the heavens, challenging Zeus' power. As a result, in the second phase of the myth Zeus intervened by cutting them in two. But the separated halves suffered and were sad. Out of pity, Zeus – and this is the third and final phase of the myth – moved their now separated genitals to the front, allowing them to couple. For this reason, every separated half searches for its lost part. Plato calls this 'pursuit of wholeness', this urge to 'restore [our] original nature', this aspiration to recompose the Original One that had undergone the offence of separation, love.[1]

This myth seems to contradict our experience of love. If the risk of the end accompanies lovers from the day of their very first encounter, it is because, even when love seems like fate, nothing can ensure it stands the test of time. The unexpected nature of the loving encounter, so full of joy and ecstasy, can suddenly tip over into the dark and dramatic unknown of detachment and demise. Love, once a balm, can become torture. It seemed like the cure for the pain of existence and now reveals itself to be the very thing making that pain more acute; it should have been the possibility of becoming 'complete', of making and being One with the Other, and instead, as Roth's protagonist of *The Dying Animal* rightly notes, causes division, 'it fractures you':

> The only obsession everyone wants: 'love.' People think that in falling in love they make themselves whole? The Platonic union of souls? I think otherwise. I think you're whole before you begin. And the love fractures you. You're whole, and then you're cracked open.[2]

If Plato believed love should heal the wound inflicted by Zeus, for Roth's anti-Platonism, love does not unify at all, but divides, fractures, cracks you in half. It divides because it exposes to us our vulnerability, highlighting the incurable nature of our lack. This is the truth that emerges, sometimes traumatically, when love comes to an end, when lovers separate. This is the time in which what was first desirable or irresistible about him or her has become unbearable or provokes indifference. The beloved is transformed into a foreign body because they have become too familiar to be desired any longer. The person to whom we are closest reveals themselves to be the furthest away. As a result, cold, conflict and desperation fall fatally upon the Two; indifference supplants dedication. Whilst in loving dedication the Other is considered unique and irreplaceable, when a love ends the same Other becomes just another among many. That body that was once the cause of my desire, that body that once secretly attracted me magnetically towards it, has become so very distant because it is far too close. All erotic contact is suspended. It looks to me like a lifeless body, an excessive presence or one that has fallen into indifference. The spell is broken:

> Toward the last, without realizing how near the end-zone was, I was still trying to puzzle out Vela, to get a handle on her motives. She preferred deeds to words, conceding that she couldn't compete with me verbally, and one day when I was reading a book (my regular diet of words) she wandered into the room entirely nude, came to my bedside and rubbed her pubic hair on my cheekbone. When I responded as she must have known that I would, she turned and left me with an air of having made her point. She had won hands down without having to speak a word. Her body spoke for her, and effectively too, saying that the end was near.[3]

The death of a love can occur through extinction or a tear. Extinction would be the natural end (if that even exists?) of the love between the Two: something has run its course, it no longer works, it has been extinguished. Love has stopped burning, it can no longer last. A tear implies the cut of separation that falls on the one of the Two who still loves, on the one of the Two who would want to continue that love, for whom that love still burns. In this case, the end of a love is not only the love of one's own Ego, which loses its fundamental support and finds itself stripped of meaning, of the meaning that love provided, but the death of the whole world, of that world of the Two miraculously born again thanks to love.

When love ends it is never only a love that comes to an end but, most importantly, the world that the Two have created. In the death of love the entire world of the Two dies along with their objects, their rituals, their memory, their travels, their restaurants, their books, their houses, the union of their bodies, their very life because the existence of love was what gave meaning to the world that is no longer.

'Separtition'

What does it mean to separate? It does not mean simply detaching from one another, putting distance between the Two, not seeing each other anymore. Separation is never an external movement, it is not comparable to detaching from someone or something. It doesn't just mean creating distance, distancing oneself, differentiating oneself. Separation is always a 'separtition' as Lacan would say.[4] It means that when we separate, we separate first and foremost with a part of ourselves, that part that was held up by the person we have lost. If I lose the person I love, I lose everything, I feel myself to be lost. It is like pulling your hand free from icy metal; something of us, a fragment of our skin, remains forever attached to the lost object, to the person who is no longer there. To separate is, therefore, to separate and partition oneself: not to lose just the Other who is no longer there, but also a piece of ourselves. This is why separations are so painful, because they rip away a part of ourselves, because when the Other moves away they take a piece of me with them. They divide me, they fracture me, they lacerate me. This is the cause of the depressive effect that accompanies every separation. Freud likens it to an emptying, a libidinal haemorrhage:[5] when leaving, the beloved Other takes with them my libido, my desire. The abandoned subject (the subject who undergoes a separation) is a libidinally impoverished subject, emptied, discarded, devalued. Not only has the world lost its meaning, but the subject itself understands how it is deprived, returned to a condition of passive defencelessness because the death of that world coincides with the death of an essential part of themselves. It is the return to life as a scream (like that depicted by Munch) that no longer finds anyone to hear its plea, no one capable of responding.

It is a sensation that often accompanies those experiencing abandonment: their life appears in its original defenceless state, a poor, insignificant, excessive thing lost in the world. More precisely: my life loses any sense, it loses meaning, because I can no longer be that which the Other is missing, I am no longer their lack, because I no longer lack, because they no longer think of me, they no longer miss me.

The pain of separation in love is a deaf and psychically indigestible pain. Without the presence of the beloved, without them listening, without the offering of their lack, I regress to the position of defenceless life. I am nothing but a scream in the night to which no one responds. No one is picking up my messages. Barthes describes the condition of finished love and separation as that of a spaceship that stops emitting signals. This is the fundamental 'mutism' that characterizes the object that once, before our separation, loved me, answered me, thought about me:

> How does a love end? – Then it does end? To tell the truth, no one – except for the others – ever knows anything about it; a kind of innocence conceals the end of this thing conceived, asserted, *lived* according to eternity. Whatever the loved being becomes, whether he vanishes or moves into the realm of Friendship, in any case I never see him disappear: the love which is over and done with passes into another world like a ship into space, lights no longer winking: the loved being once echoed loudly, now that being is entirely without resonance (the other never disappears when and how we expect).[6]

If the silence of the beloved appears unbearable it is because it strongly signals that its presence has irreversibly transformed into an absence. No one returns to me the love that I can offer. My declaration of love ('I love you') no longer has a recipient. Like a ghost ship, I go back to floating through nothingness. I no longer have value because I am no longer missed by anyone, because there is no one that thinks of me. The end of love is the end of a thought that thinks of me, of someone listening who answers me. I am no longer their lack. The Other can live without me. In the place of their presence falls the shadow of their absence.

Destinies of Separation

Every separation implies mourning. This was a real enigma for Freud: why is the libido of the one who finds themselves alone not able to immediately substitute the lost object with another? Why doesn't it work towards swiftly finding a replacement? If the drive is concerned only with one's own satisfaction, why does it waste time crying over the lost object, feeling the pain of its loss? In other words, Freud believed the enigma of mourning lies in the libido's lingering not on an object's presence (as would be logical) but on its absence, on the loss of the object.[7] Why doesn't the libido spontaneously go back to being invested in the world rather than remaining stubbornly attached to the lost object?

The work of mourning is necessary to detach the subject from the shadow of the lost object. Each time love ends the subject takes up the inevitable work of mourning. How can we live again after the death of a love? After having undergone the tear of this loss? How can we love again? The absence of the person who is no longer there can become an oppressive presence ('All I can think about is their absence; I miss them so much; my life has no meaning without them'). The work of mourning is necessary in order to free oneself from this ever-present absence.

It is a painful work that takes time, psychical pain and memory. More than anything else it needs time. There is no such thing as fast mourning. The psychical time of mourning is needed not to forget the object, but to go back over our life with them, to remember the love that was. There is no possibility of forgetting without remembering. This work is particularly painful because the beloved object is no longer with us, they have left us, taking with them a part of us and leaving our lives empty. This work serves to reclaim the libido absorbed by the Other. Only at the end of this work of memory will we be able to forget the lost object and recover our libido, which will be available once more to be invested in other objects.

Today, however, there is no end of easier, less painful alternatives to the necessarily lengthy work of mourning. One of these is the maniacal replacement of the object: rather than dealing with the wound of the loss, rather than remembering lost love, it is better to sew that wound up as quickly as possible with a new object. It is better to forget. This forgetting is not, however, achieved by the work of memory but with the substitution of the object. Today's world encourages this maniacal solution to mourning: one love is dead? Then another must immediately take its place. Our times are hostile to the 'unproductive' and 'painful' experience of mourning, dominated instead by the neo-libertine injunction to enjoy at all costs. The self-reflection required by the work of mourning appears entirely anachronistic. Better to incentivize the immediate substitution of the object preached by the capitalist discourse.

If separation throws both the meaning of my Ego and the world itself into freefall, the first way of protecting myself from the anxiety provoked by the separation is to replace the lost object with a new one. To find in another bond the balm required to soothe the wound left by love. But it is unlikely for a loving encounter to happen if the presence of the object's absence still weighs so heavy; if the necessary work of mourning has not taken place. In order to encounter a new presence, we must make sure that the absence is a real one, first psychically burying the person who is no longer here in order to be open to a new encounter. Another possible and rather frequent outcome of separation, an alternative to mourning, is that of hate. If the separation is experienced as a betrayal of the pact, as a narcissistic wound, as violence or as offence, it is common for that old love to be overwhelmed by hate. Sometimes this hate can take the dramatic form of real violence and persecution that aims to deny the Other the freedom to leave, to say 'goodbye'. The hate that does not manifest itself as enacted violence is an operation aimed at destroying the beloved object. It is the upturning of idealization: if in love we only saw the beauty, the generosity, the charm of the beloved object, now we only see their limits and imperfections. If the Other no longer loves me I must destroy their image, which has become a source of pain, or their very life, which does sometimes dramatically happen. The tragic illusion, however, is that of separating from the one who has left me using hate, taking the path of destruction and death, without understanding that hate is never a true movement of separation. Where there is hate, there is always an attachment, albeit in a negative form, to the lost object. Hate always tends to stick the subject to the person who has been loved and is now no longer there. Essentially, it is used in order to avoid taking the tortuous path of the work of mourning. This is why Lacan is able to say that hate is a 'career without limit':[8] it has no peace, no limit, no end and no satisfaction.

The dramatic observation that makes itself clear at this point is that, while in love the Other became the person who created a lack in me, who created an inevitable form of dependency for me, that love can always carry with it the possibility of hate: it was better before, before when I didn't lack anything, before the arrival of your existence in my life. You arrived and a hole opened up in the world and in me, perforating it, destabilizing it. My life has been smashed to pieces, divided, broken. It is better, then, to construct a world without the Other. This is the reactive plan that often accompanies the wounds caused by love. It happens with the strange animal protagonist in one of Kafka's short stories, 'The Burrow'.[9] He decides to live far from everyone, under the ground, safe from the treachery of the world. He builds his burrow like a fortress that protects him and separates him from the Other. He wants to destroy any possibility of encounter with the Other's desire, he wants to be left alone. His house becomes an impregnable bunker built like a labyrinth that only he is able to navigate. Many aspire to this: in order to avoid the wound of love, or to mend it and ensure that it never opens again, it is better to avoid any kind of relationship with the Other, better not to get involved with the Other's desire, better to live hidden underground. One of my patients told me of an extraordinary lapsus. Right in the middle of her morning Our Father, instead of saying 'do not lead us into temptation', she eloquently says 'and free us from the relation'. The life of the One closed in itself is always less laborious and turbulent than that of the Two. It doesn't involve risk, or the threat of wounds. The protagonist of Kafka's short story prefers solitude and isolation to the possibility of the encounter, fleeing from the bond with the Other as if from leprosy. He is convinced that he has done away with the danger of the Other once and for all. In truth, however, the Other suddenly reappears in the form of a whistle, at first almost imperceptible and then increasingly pervasive, heralding its destabilizing presence. The animal's desperate attempts to protect itself from the threat of this whistle's constant presence as it grows nearer are in vain. It cannot escape the relationship with the Other's unknown.

7

Enduring Love

The poem to duration is a love poem.
It is about love at first sight
followed by many such first sights.

Peter Handke, *To Duration*[1]

To Burn or To Last?

Does all love end badly? Are all loves destined to lose their initial power, to wither and die, to decay into submission and become cemeteries for desire? Isn't this what experience tells us? All that is left is affection and the memory of what has been. Is love perhaps like Caravaggio's *Basket of Fruit* (1594–8), in which the barely noticeable presence of a rotten apple among the impressively presented fruit announces the fatal corruption of life? Love that burns does not know how to last precisely because desire imposes the continual replacement of the object as a condition of its existence. The push towards the New incinerates the Same, revealing it as the place where desire meets its death. Our time has made a universal law of Freud's thesis on the common degradation of neurotics' love life, characterized by the incompatibility of the tenderness able to stand the test of time and the sensual current of desire that demands the object always be new: if there is love, there is no desire; if there is desire, there is no love.

And yet we know that love does exist in which that initial gaze never ceases to repeat itself, in which the first sight and the first kiss continue to be always new despite being the same. Love exists where that kiss is maintained. In short, there is love capable of lasting, love that defies the theory of the inversely proportional relationship between the intensity of desire and how long it lasts. There is love that wants to subvert the cynical assertion that every love must end in the shit. There are glorious, everyday loves that do not want to die, that bet on the possibility of holding together both burning and lasting. They are not so very different to those that die after burning and after having done everything possible in order to last.

Love that lasts contains the essence of love. It is a miracle that cannot explain why desire's most proper tendency is to pit burning against lasting. A general observation can, however, be made: loves that last are those in which each of the Two is comfortable with their own loneliness. This means that the loving bond is not so much the balm that heals the wound of solitude, but the encounter between two solitudes. This is why Lacan, when defining the loving encounter, uses the image of an encounter between two exiles.[2] Because love that lasts is not based in any way on the proximity between or fusion of the Two, but on distance, on the unshareability, on the impossibility of making and being One with the Other. It is based on the solitude of the Two. Love that lasts is not a love that is entirely consumed by passion for the beloved, that knows no plan other than that of burning together, but nor is it the love that unifies, that identifies, that confuses One with the Other. The existence of the beloved is an unknown that can never be fully translated: their heart, which I feel in my own, remains theirs, their body, which I feel in my own, remains different from mine, their life, which I feel united with my own, is never mine.

The Intimacy of Strangers

Love burns when desire lights the bodies. How long will it last? The life of the Two that knows how to endure does not exclude eroticism in any way. The everyday life of a shared existence does not necessarily imply the familiarization of the Other. The breath of desire is always possible in the life of every couple if love continues to exist:

> You're 82 years old. You've shrunk six centimetres, you only weigh 45 kilos yet you're still beautiful, graceful and desirable. We've lived together now for 58 years and I love you more than ever. I once more feel a gnawing emptiness in the hollow of my chest that is only filled when your body is pressed next to mine [. . .] You've just turned 82. You're still beautiful, graceful and desirable. We've lived together now for 58 years and I love you more than ever. Lately I've fallen in love with you all over again and I once more feel a gnawing emptiness inside that can only be filled when your body is pressed against mine. At night I sometimes see the figure of a man, on an empty road in a deserted

landscape, walking behind the hearse. I am that man. It is you the hearse is taking away.[3]

The author of these words is André Gorz. He describes his love for his wife just after they have decided to end their own lives together because of a serious illness that has afflicted his beloved. Their bond is one of love that has known how to stand the test of time. In this dramatic farewell, his desire is evoked with love and not against it. She forever remains 'beautiful, graceful and desirable'. Time, in this case, has neither cooled nor killed desire. Rather, love has suspended time, or even better, it has made time love's friend and not its enemy. Love has not diminished over time, but grown. Their bodies held close to one another press pause on the pain of the world, a break from the 'gnawing emptiness' of life. Without the shared experience of the wound it is difficult for love to exist.

There is no love that does not feed on lack. Lacan says it in his own way with a now famous formula: to love means giving the Other that which one does not have.[4] This means that in love I will not limit myself to giving the Other what I possess, things, objects, security, prospects, income; the most proper gift of love is that of our lack, it is the gift of our wound. Lovers are a break from the pain of the world, as Berger wrote. This break is a joy that can be renewed over time, one that can last. So, the repetition of the same love does not kill desire but renews it. Love saves us each time from the wound of the world.

Our time tends to compare the effervescent life of the New with the dull grey of the Same. It wrongly maintains that the

Same is the death of the New. It takes from this that a couple's desire will have a brief lifespan, that its days are numbered. Like those of a fridge or a television destined soon to be substituted by updated, more efficient models. Our time thinks of love as belonging to the category of 'commodities'. Its fetishism, the fetishism of commodities, as Marx explained, misrecognized the significance of endurance. It burns itself up, it consumes itself starting with the offering of other objects that the laws of the market endlessly place at our disposal.

Desire is never content with what it has; it is always looking at what it does not. As Lacan once said, it is like Bruegel's *Parable of the Blind* (1568):[5] desire is a perpetual movement that cannot find peace in any object. It comes and goes, wandering from one object to the next. The blindness of desire lies in the unrestrained quest for a new partner, and the belief that in the New it will find its true satisfaction. In reality, desire consumes every object, making it old, obsolete, like commodities that have completed their function and been replaced by more efficient object-commodities. Desire is blind because it tends to oppose the New to the Same; it does not know how to imagine that the real face of the New is just a different fold of the Same, and not the New opposed to the Same.

In opposition to this worship of the New that only produces the same dissatisfaction is the endurance that makes every single thing truly different. It is not the New versus the Same, but the New in the Same, it is the New as an internal fold of the Same. Indeed, love is the possibility of elevating an object to the position of one that is not just another in a series, but that is irreplaceable, incomparable, unique. Love elevates that foot, that hand, that face, that smell, that voice, giving it the dignity of an object that is incomparable, irreplaceable, unique, thus disrupting desire's slide from one object to another.

Within this is the possibility of uniting desire with enjoyment, of welding the Name to the body, making of the body a Name and of the Name a body. The infinite number of steps that Montale descends with his woman are a possible symbol of endurance: 'I have walked, with you on my arm, down at least a million steps.'[6] The same arm, the same steps, but each time the first arm and the first steps. This is the intimacy of strangers that must not be confused with that alienating intimacy that Adorno talks of in *Minima Moralia*, with his reference to the symbol of the father's white vest during the summer months.[7]

Intimacy in love that lasts does not dissolve the mystery of the body. It does not allow itself to be stolen from the familiar. On the contrary: the repetition of the Same, rather than destroying the New, feeds it. The body whose geography, curves, elevations, depths and consistency I know by heart is always made new by the unstoppable passing of time. This is the miracle of love when it lasts: not being in opposition to desire but being that which makes the object of desire unique and irreplaceable, that which lights its flames.

In these loves, faithfulness is not the fruit of sacrifice, but intoxication, vertigo, the insistence of a force, of an enigma, of a mystery. Faithfulness, when it is the expression of a living love, excludes surrender or resignation as a matter of principle. Otherwise it becomes a sacrificial illness, a straitjacket for desire. Mystery lies in the beauty of endurance. It is Odysseus' act, which struck me as a child and continues to do so with ever-greater force: how could he prefer his Penelope to the beautiful, young Calypso? But, most of all, how could he have chosen a woman marked by time over the endless beauty of immortality? What madness is love if it leads a man to renounce eternal life? Wasn't this Odysseus' most fascinating act of madness? Is it not madness that leads him to decline the nymph's offer?

> Mighty goddess, be not wroth with me for this. I know full well of myself that wise Penelope is meaner to look upon than thou in comeliness and in stature, for she is a mortal, while thou art immortal and ageless. But even so I wish and long day by day to reach my home, and to see the day of my return.[8]

The Two is not an empathetic jam, an undifferentiated identification, an intimacy without desire, but a relationship between non-equals, a shared experience of the unshareable, 'stellar friendship' as Nietzsche would have it, *the intimacy of strangers*. This is love's greatest duty, its real work: to make desire last *over* time, for Eros and the encounter to endure *over* time. This is the profound mystery at the *intersection between transience and eternity*. When this happens it is marvellous, a true miracle. But there are no recipes, courses, techniques, or experts to guide us. We only know that it sometimes happens. For Camus it would only happen a maximum of three times a century,[9] and one of those was for him, so he doesn't leave us much hope.

At First Sight, Once More

The bodies of lovers change over time; they change shape, colour, consistency, character. Duration, however, does not consume but renews. It does not move away from its origin, but carries its origin with it, in the insistence of its repetition. The length of the duration is not a corruption of the present, it is not death or degradation but a renewal of its beginnings. It is love's most proper miracle, when it exists: making the Same, New. Repetition does not destroy love but makes it infinite:

The poem to duration is a love poem.
It is about love at first sight
followed by many such first sights.
And this love,
its duration not in any deed,
much more in a before and after –
through love's altered sense of time
the before was also after
and the after also before.
We had already become one
before we had become one,
continued to become
after we had become one,
and lay that way for years,
hip to hip, breath to breath,
side by side.

Your brown hair reddened
then turned blond.
Your proliferating scars
became untraceable.
Your voice trembled,
became firm, whispered, quavered,
fell into singsong,
the only sound in the worldwide night,
was silent, next to me.
Your straight hair curled,
your bright eyes darkened,
your large teeth grew smaller,
the taut skin of your lips
developed a fine, lightly drawn pattern,
on your always smooth chin
I felt an unfamiliar indentation,
and our bodies, instead of wounding,
joined playfully into one,
while on the wall of the room
in the street lantern light
there was a shadowy shifting of European shrubs,
the shadows of American trees
the shadows of nightbirds from everywhere.[10]

Everything about your body changes, writes Handke, but as it changes it renews the 'first sight' of the encounter and its promise. There are no other sights or kisses after the first ones. The first kisses and first sights do not just fade over time. There is not just the memory of that first sight, that first kiss, because they always endure in the present. Endurance is not an unhappy distancing from the origin, nor is it an extinguishing of the initial flame, but the possibility for the beginning to always be new once more.

Endurance upends our ordinary understanding of the time of love: there is no beginning – the time of the encounter – from which we inevitably move away, its intensity fatally fading. The passing of time does not necessarily imply the corruption and degradation of the origin. Rather (and this is the miracle of endurance), that same origin is renewed in every moment because it is in the present, in our most ordinary daily present – in the now – that the possibility of other first sights is always present. The first sight is not simply the gaze that has already been, in the past, behind me, behind us, from which we irreversibly distance ourselves, but it is the gaze that never ceases to be that first sight.

The enchantment, the miracle of endurance is that this gaze (first sight like the first kiss) can happen again, again once more. It is no coincidence that for Lacan the first word of love, the fundamental cell of every loving discourse, is the word 'again', *encore*.[11] Again, again like today, again like now. Again is the word that lovers use with one another: 'Stay, I want more, again once more, stay again.' Again, for Lacan, is the fundamental word of love. The beloved asks for love to be again, they ask that there be love again, that the face of the beloved remains, that the life of love will again be like it is today, once again like it is now. Again is the word that makes new that love capable of lasting and burning at the same time: again is the most profound word of endurance.

In this sense, as Handke writes, we can continue to unite ourselves after already being united, we can discover wounds in our own bodies that we had not yet seen. We cannot hurt one another, but we can make our room, our 'hiding place', our conspiracy bigger, enlarge that 'hiding place', that conspiracy between the Two in order to further dilate the horizon of the world until it includes, as the poet writes, all of Europe, America and 'everywhere'.

Notes

Chapter 1   The Promise

1 Roland Barthes, *A Lover's Discourse: Fragments*, Penguin, London 1979, p. 23.

2 For more on this, see S. Regazzoni, *Ti amo: Filosofia come dichiarazione d'amore* [*I Love You: Philosophy as a Declaration of Love*], Utet, Milan 2017.

3 See Darian Leader, *Promises Lovers Make When It Gets Late*, Faber and Faber, London 1998.

4 Barthes, *Lover's Discourse*, p. 119.

5 Jacques Lacan, *Talking to Brick Walls*, Polity, Cambridge 2017.

6 See Jacques Lacan, *The Seminar of Jacques Lacan: Book X*, Polity, Cambridge 2014, p. 337.

7 Pablo Neruda, 'One Hundred Love Sonnets: XVII', in *The Essential Neruda: Selected Poems*, ed. Mark Eisner, City Lights Books, San Francisco 2004.

8 Karl Ove Knausgård, *A Man in Love: My Struggle. Book 2*, tr. Don Bartlett, Vintage, London 2013, p. 153.

9 Jean-Paul Sartre, *Being and Nothingness: An Essay in Phenomenological Ontology*, Routledge, Abingdon 2018, p. 371.

10 These are the words Maria Schneider says to Marlon Brando in

Last Tango in Paris (1972) by Bernardo Bertolucci. See Jacques Lacan, *The Seminar of Jacques Lacan: Book XX*, W. W. Norton, New York 1999, and Alain Badiou, *In Praise of Love*, Profile Books, London 2012.

11 Homer, *Odyssey*, XXIII, 177–98.

Chapter 2 Desire

1 Philip Roth, *The Dying Animal*, Vintage, London 2016, p. 16.

2 'Every kind of love, however ethereal it may seem to be, springs entirely from the instinct of sex; indeed, it is absolutely this instinct, only in a more definite, specialised, and perhaps, strictly speaking, more individualised form.' See Arthur Schopenhauer, 'Metaphysics of Sexual Love', in *World as Will and Representation. Vol. II*, Falcon's Wing Press, Indian Hills 1958, pp. 531–67.

3 Salter, *Sport and a Pastime*, pp. 180–1.

4 Paul Éluard, *Le dur désir de durer* [*The Firm Desire to Endure*], in *Last Love Poems of Paul Eluard*, Black Widow Press, Boston 2006.

5 Philip Roth, *The Professor of Desire*, Vintage, London 2016, pp. 22–3.

6 Lacan, *Seminar: Book XX*, p. 12.

7 John Berger and Marc Trivier, *My Beautiful*, Italian tr. M. Nadotti, Bruno Mondadori, Milan 2008, p. 38, translated from the Italian.

Chapter 3 Children

1 Emmanuel Lévinas, *Totality and Infinity: An Essay on Exteriority*, Kluwer, Dordrecht 1991, p. 279.

2 Mariangela Gualtieri, 'Canto di ferro' ['Song of Iron'], in *Paesaggio con fratello rotto* [*Landscape with a Broken Brother*], Luca Sossella Editore, Rome 2007.

3 Jacques Deleuze and Félix Guattari, *Anti-Oedipus*, Bloomsbury, London 2013.

4 See Lévinas, *Totality and Infinity*, pp. 278–81.

5 See Massimo Recalcati, *The Son's Secret: From Oedipus to the Prodigal Son*, Polity, Cambridge 2020.

6 On the opposition of these two economies, I would refer you to Massimo Recalcati, *Contro il sacrificio: Al di là del fantasma sacrificale* [*Against Sacrifice: Beyond the Sacrificial Fantasy*], Raffaello Cortina, Milan 2017.

7 I refer you to Massimo Recalcati, *The Mother's Hands: Desire, Fantasies and Inheritance of the Maternal*, Polity, Cambridge 2019.

Chapter 4 Betrayal and Forgiveness

1 Marcel Proust, *In Search of Lost Time. Vol. 5: The Captive*, Modern Library, New York 1982, p. 82.

2 Alberto Moravia, *Boredom*, New York Review of Books, New York 1999, p. 154.

3 Moravia, *Boredom*, p. 157.

4 Barthes, *Lover's Discourse*, p. 35.

5 Moravia, *Boredom*, pp. 211–12.

6 Jean Améry, *At the Mind's Limits: Contemplations by a Survivor on Auschwitz and its Realities*, Indiana University Press, Bloomington 1980, pp. 27–8.

7 I refer you here to my book, Massimo Recalcati, *In Praise of Forgiveness*, Polity, Cambridge 2020.

8 Jacques Derrida, *On Cosmopolitanism and Forgiveness*, Routledge, London 1997.

Chapter 5 Violence

1 Sartre, *Being and Nothingness*, p. 534.

2 M. Sgorbani, 'Blondi (il cane di Hitler)' ['Hitler's Dog'], in *Innamorate dello spavento* [*In Love with Fear*], Titivillus, Pisa 2013, pp. 18–19.

3 Sartre, *Being and Nothingness*, p. 383.

4 Moravia, *Boredom*, p. 146.

5 Proust, *In Search of Lost Time. Vol. 5*, pp. 75–6.

6 Barthes, *Lover's Discourse*, p. 71.

7 Barthes, *Lover's Discourse*, p. 14.

8 Elena Ferrante, *My Brilliant Friend*, Europa Editions, New York 2012, pp. 52–3.

9 See Sigmund Freud, 'Analysis Terminable and Interminable', in *The Standard Edition of the Complete Psychological Works of Sigmund Freud. Vol. XXIII (1937–1939): Moses and Monotheism, An Outline of Psychoanalysis and Other Works*, Vintage, London 2001, pp. 209–54.

10 Lacan, *Seminar: Book XX*, p. 7.

11 Sgorbani, 'Blondi (il cane di Hitler)', p. 41.

Chapter 6 Separations

1 Plato, *The Symposium*, Penguin, London 1999, pp. 26–7.
2 Roth, *Dying Animal*, p. 99.
3 Saul Bellow, *Ravelstein*, Penguin, New York 2000, p. 86.
4 See Lacan, *Seminar: Book X*, p. 237.
5 See Sigmund Freud, 'Mourning and Melancholia', in *The Standard Edition of the Complete Psychological Works of Sigmund Freud. Vol. XIV (1914–1916): On the History of the Psycho-Analytic Movement, Papers on Metapsychology and Other Works*, Vintage, London 2001, pp. 237–58.
6 Barthes, *Lover's Discourse*, p. 101.
7 See Freud, 'Mourning and Melancholia'.
8 Jacques Lacan, *The Seminar of Jacques Lacan: Book I*, W. W. Norton, London 1991, p. 277.
9 Franz Kafka, 'The Burrow', in *The Burrow and Other Stories*, Penguin, London 2017.

Chapter 7 Enduring Love

1 Peter Handke, *To Duration*, tr. Scott Abbott, Last Books, Amsterdam 2015, p. 21.
2 Lacan, *Seminar: Book XX*, p. 145.
3 André Gorz, *Letter to D: A Love Story*, tr. Julie Rose, Polity, Cambridge 2009, pp. 1 and 105–6.
4 See Jacques Lacan, *The Seminar of Jacques Lacan: Book V*, Polity, Cambridge 2017, p. 194.
5 Jacques Lacan, 'Kant with Sade', in *Écrits: The First Complete*

Edition in English, tr. Bruce Fink, W. W. Norton, London 2006, p. 785.

6 Eugenio Montale, 'Ho sceso, dandoti il braccio, almeno un milione di scale' ['I have walked with you on my arm, down at least a million steps'], in *Satura*, Mondadori, Milan 2018.

7 T. W. Adorno, *Minima Moralia: Reflections on a Damaged Life*, Verso, London 2005, pp. 181–2.

8 Homer, *Odyssey*, V, 215–20. I recently had the opportunity to revisit Odysseus' 'madness' in Massimo Recalcati, *A libro aperto: Una vita è i suoi libri* [*An Open Book: A Life and Its Books*], Feltrinelli, Milan 2018, pp. 71–9.

9 'Of course, true love is the exception – roughly two or three instances in a century': Albert Camus, *The Fall*, Penguin, London 2006, p. 360.

10 Handke, *To Duration*, p. 21.

11 Lacan, *Seminar: Book XX*.